John Tuccillo, Bu

TARGETING THE
Over 55 Client

Your Guide to

Today's Fastest Growing Market

**Real Estate
Education Company**
a division of Dearborn Financial Publishing, Inc.

Acquisitions Editor: Christine E. Litavsky
Managing Editor: Jack Kiburz
Associate Project Editor: Stephanie C. Schmidt
Interior Design: Lucy Jenkins
Cover Design: David Corona Design

© 1995 by Dearborn Financial Publishing, Inc.®

Published by Real Estate Education Company,®
a division of Dearborn Financial Publishing, Inc.®

Printed in the United States of America

95 96 97 10 9 8 7 6 5 4 3 2 1

Library of Congress Cataloging-in-Publication Data

Tuccillo, John A.
    Targeting the over-55 client : your guide to today's fastest
growing market / John Tuccillo, Buddy West, Betsy West.
        p.   cm.
    Includes index.
    ISBN 0-7931-1318-0 (pbk.)
    1. Real estate business—United States.   2. Aged as consumers—
United States.   3. Aged—Housing—United States.   4. House selling—
United States.   5. Real estate business—United States—Marketing.
    I. West, Buddy.   II. West, Betsy.   III. Title
    HD259.T83   1995
333.33′068′8—dc20   95-17975
                                                                CIP

Dedication

This book is for all the seniors in our lives, but particularly for Ethel West (July 4, 1921–December 9, 1994) whose housing circumstances inspired Buddy's commitment to this book, but who could not be here to see the finished work.

Contents

Preface   vii

Acknowledgments   ix

Chapter 1. Disovering the Profitable Over-55 Market   1

Chapter 2. Zeroing In on the Importance of the Over-55 Marketplace   7

Chapter 3. Winning Credibility with Compassion   21

Chapter 4. Understanding the Way It Was   27

Chapter 5. Considerations When Listing with the Seasoned Citizen   33

Chapter 6. Navigating the Road to Sold   43

Chapter 7. Teaming Up for Success   51

Chapter 8. Emphasizing Old Rules, Explaining New Ones   65

Chapter 9. Financing Options for the Over-55 Market   73

Chapter 10. Building Tomorrow's Business by Helping Them Stay Today   81

Chapter 11. Finding and Capturing the Older Market   89

Chapter 12. A Menu of Materials To Ensure Success   97

Appendix A. State Agencies on Housing and Aging   133

Appendix B. State Housing Finance Authorities   147

Appendix C. Reverse Mortgage Lenders List   151

Appendix D. FannieMae Seniors' Housing Opportunities   169

Index   177

Preface

Real estate has always been a niche business. Most successful real estate professionals have specialized in a certain corner of the market, whether it be a geographic area, a type of dwelling or a particular price range. The first-time buyer market, in particular, has been a popular road to success. But now, with demographic shifts concentrating the population of the United states in older age brackets, the last-time homebuyer may become the fastest growing market segment and a new niche for the professional.

The over-55 age group will be growing at about twice the rate of the population as a whole. Although no single profile will describe this entire group, it's safe to say that compared to their predecessors, they are smarter and wealthier. While their sheer numbers alone make them an attractive real estate niche, their buying power and housing sophistication open up a whole range of new business possibilities. This is indeed a potentially lucrative market.

There have been many books written about every real estate submarket, as well as general books on listing, selling, financing, advertising and working with clients and customers. However, there has been little available to guide the real estate professional into and through the senior housing market. This book will show you how to prospect and service that market and thus establish a reputation for expertise in dealing with a truly remarkable and fast-growing segment of the real estate market.

Acknowledgments

This book stems from the experiences and training of the authors, but could not have been born without considerable help from a significant number of people. We begin by thanking Kate Anderson, whose guidance, research assistance and editorial eye shaped this work to the point where she is, in effect, an uncredited coauthor.

We also owe a debt of gratitude to the many members of the real estate, legal and senior citizen communities for lending their technical advice. From real estate, we'd like to thank Pat Zaby, a nationally recognized real estate educator and creator of Prep™ Presentations; Randy Purcell, creator of Top Producer® software; Mary Charters (RE/MAX, Gaithersburg, Maryland); and Martha Sell (Coldwell Banker, Marietta, Georgia). Each graciously provided perspectives on the senior real estate market. Laura Dietz, Buddy and Betsy's assistant, provided a great help in crafting the case studies.

On the legal side, we thank Donald C. Taylor (Cooch and Taylor, Wilmington, Delaware), Jonathan Taylor (Taylor and Gruver, Wilmington) and Gail Ahrens (General Counsel, Patterson Schwartz and Co., Hockessin, Delaware), who all guided us through the legal maze surrounding the older market. James Selsor (Barbacane Thornton and Co., Wilmington) helped us with accounting issues. From a financial perspective, our thanks to Phyllis

Wilson, a loan originator at Gilpin Financial, Wilmington, Delaware. And Mary Jane Nikolich (The Resettlers, Inc., Centerville, Delaware) and Sally E. Williams (Executive Director, Mid-County Senior Center, Inc., Wilmington) helped us greatly in our understanding of the psychology of older Americans.

Chapter 1

Discovering the Profitable Over-55 Market

Experience in the real estate business has shown us that one year will never be the same as the previous year, and each year presents new and different markets. Success for REALTORS® depends on their ability to be in the Eden of emerging markets.

Historically, the real estate practitioner has created a business targeted to specific markets identified by the position of buyers on the housing ladder, their geographic areas or both. The most important segment has been the first rung on the ladder: the first-time homeseller. Because this group is highly motivated and actively seeks home ownership, it is always worth the time and effort to cultivate. Working with first-time homesellers requires that the agent have patience, perseverance and the ability to coach the buyer through the homebuying process.

The largest markets occupy the next few rungs up the ladder in the form of the move-up buyer. For the real estate agent, this type of household presents opportunities for both the buying and the selling sides of the real estate transaction, a double dip if you please. The number of move-up buyers is often determined by the strength of the economy. When the housing market is strong, you will find a large number of move-up buyers; when the market is weak, the move-up buyers stay put.

The move-up buyers of the 1990s may move up more than once. Family recomposition and job shifting may result in "move-around" buyers as well. If you've worked in the real estate industry over the last ten years or so you've seen the impact of divorce on homes sold and moves made. Divorce and financial insecurity have contributed to the merging of households by different generations as well. Today, moves are as often lateral as up.

All of these profiles make legitimate business sources for our industry and warrant pursuit.

The Last Rung on the Ladder

Of all the markets on the ladder of home ownership, none presents a greater opportunity than the last-time homesellers. This said, it makes good business sense to explore and understand the fastest growing and potentially wealthiest segment of our population: the over-55s. They are predominantly homeowners (over 70 percent), aware of the value of professional advice and probably beginning to retire and relocate. Over the next ten years, their numbers will grow by millions. Now, that's a market!

As the baby boom goes into its senior years, the ranks of these "new elderly" will increase dramatically. This generation will be the most experienced and affluent generation of seniors in American history. They have regularly worked outside the home, are better educated than their predecessors and on average have moved twice as frequently as the previous generation.

The over-55 market, like any other, comes with its own set of challenges. As a group they have even been described as difficult. Why? Perhaps because conventional wisdom says the following:

- These people are hard to please.
- They are distrustful and hard to approach.
- They resist change.
- Their homes are dated.
- They are out of touch with reality.

Granted, older citizens bring a lifetime of experiences that converge to color reactions and responses to you and the task at hand. Frequently, also, something about the sellers or their situation is less than ideal, both from their standpoint and yours. But these citizens are not homogeneous; they are a most diverse group. There is some question about whether they can be segmented, defined and profiled (sufficiently so that a REALTOR® can determine the efforts necessary to target this market successfully).

Remember, though, the rich and diverse makeup of this group, and that those moving into the population will have even less in common with those now defining the group. Be slow to stereotype, accepting of limitations and always ready to appreciate exceptions to the rule.

So why should the seasoned market be perceived as difficult? Because it can be. Recognize that it is a potentially challenging group that when worked properly can offer a REALTOR® many years of success. It is also a market that will never disappear and in fact will grow larger.

Slices of Life

Conventional wisdom went out the window when we met the Bawms. Every REALTOR® welcomes a call like the one we got from Mr. Bawm that November. He was interested in our services to sell his house. To make good news even better, the house was located in an affluent neighborhood with a good resale history.

We did our usual prelisting preparation and were off to pursue new business. Mr. and Mrs. Bawm proved to be an attractive, sophisticated pair of perfectionists. We learned that in addition to selling their house, they were also in the process of building a lakefront home in the mountains of Pennsylvania and owned real estate on the coasts of Florida and Delaware. The Bawms now had less need of their large home in our town. They wanted to replace it with a more manageable townhouse in the area—one that they could use as a business base and for periodic visits to the area.

The Bawms' situation presented us with a number of possibilities as REALTORS®. There was a house and additional lot to be sold for just under half a million dollars as well as a townhouse in the range of $150,000 to be purchased. Opportunity was literally pounding on our door!

The home to be sold was an elegant reflection of its owners. Although some 30 years old, it had received very practical and attractive additions, its systems were of top quality and updated throughout, and the custom decorating would, for the most part, be appealing to the potential buyer. The adjoining lot would be appealing to either the purchaser of the Bawms' home or one of the many buyers eager for a nice lot on which to build a new home.

Within several months the Bawms' handsome home and lot had been sold and they had purchased a townhome for $140,000. The gross volume of the combined transactions totaled just over $615,000. This translated into commissions totaling in excess of $40,000 to our broker and a large sum of that directly to us. Why can't we find more clients like this?

Are these sellers/buyers unique? Beyond their seasoned citizen status, the Bawms defied conventional wisdom. Though in their 70s, they were approachable, accepted us as professionals and listened to our advice. In short order, they treated us as friends, though we had never met before the listing appointment. They were reasonable with regard to the staging of their home and allowing access for showings. They were not resistant to change, at least not with regard to moving their primary home. They were selling a large home to move to a smaller one, acting to keep their lives manageable while still maintaining their lifestyle.

Though overseeing custom construction some distance away and following progress of the new townhome nearby, the Bawms showed little evidence of stress and no sign of second-guessing their decision. Mrs. Bawm handled a myriad of details in person and by phone and both Bawms eagerly anticipated enjoying their mountain retreat. Just keeping up with the Bawms took some doing.

These sellers were clearly aware of market conditions, as evidenced by their cooperation in positioning their home for sale and their willingness in negotiating the asking price after just a brief period. They acknowledged that the market had indeed shifted as other personal investments were also being affected.

Dealing with the Bawms taught us a valuable lesson: older citizens cannot be stereotyped as a group. They need to be treated as any other client. Agents should not prejudge the seasoned citizen as someone who needs to be spoken to in a louder voice or who can only read large-print material.

In many cases, the REALTOR® *may* have to go the extra mile to ensure that the client fully understands the process of buying and selling a home. This is not because the client/customer doesn't understand the process, but because of the time elapsed since their last transaction and how the process has changed over those years. In just the last ten years, the process of selling a home has produced a third more paperwork to be read, understood and signed or acknowledged. Think about how much the process has multiplied in the last 40 years. In the 1950s, property disclosure and agency disclosure were unheard of; in the 1990s, both are mandatory. It is our job as professional REALTORS® to explain these changes, large and small, in a clear, understandable way without making the client feel out of touch or incapable.

The differences between market niches lie mostly in how one approaches them. All markets can be difficult but can become easier with the understanding that comes with knowledge and practice. We hope to give you that knowledge so that you can practice effectively. We want to help you to tap into this older market by guiding you through the steps needed to ensure a trouble-free and profitable relationship.

It is instructive to draw a parallel between the first-time homeseller and the last-time homeseller. The first-time homeseller usually insists on being involved in every aspect of the sale in order to learn the procedure. The last-time homeseller also wants involvement, but for different reasons. Often older households don't wish to give up any control over the outcome of the sale before (until) they feel comfortable and trust you. First-timers frequently rely on parents for guidance when purchasing property. Older sellers may seek assurance from a trusted adviser that they are doing the right thing. Last-time homesellers often rely on a child or trusted professional to help them make decisions.

The Good News about the Over-55 Market

Simply looking at the size of the over-55 market and its projected growth justifies giving this group serious consideration as a target business source. If you are persuaded, the following chapters will help to reinforce your interest. They will help you to better appreciate this divergent market, empathize with older clients and adapt your tools and talents to better meet their needs.

The most successful agents position themselves in front of an emerging market. This book is about just that: offering you ways to position yourself successfully. This is an exciting time in the housing market and working with seasoned clients is going to be a rewarding experience. Let's jump in and do it; we'll be more helpful, and more successful, than ever!

Chapter 2

Zeroing In on the Importance of the Over-55 Marketplace

Okay, let's answer the basic question first. What's in this market for me? The seasoned customer is not usually considered a profit center. The conventional wisdom is that older clients are difficult to deal with, live in homes that are harder to sell, yield lower commissions and are generally not looking to buy. That's conventional wisdom.

But like a lot of beliefs in the real estate business today, this one is becoming more myth than reality. As the population ages, growing numbers of sophisticated Americans, who have built considerable home equity and other wealth after long careers in responsible jobs, are about to reenter the housing market for the first time in decades.

The stereotypical older seller remains: the one who still requires a great deal of care and handholding. But that stereotype is fading as this market is replaced by sellers who look little different from your current clients. In fact, in many cases they have been your clients in the past. In short, this is a market which is underserved and potentially as lucrative as your mainstream business.

Finding and "owning" niches in the real estate market has always made good sense. It has enabled practitioners to use their time and knowledge more efficiently and often gain respect, recognition and an identity for specific expertise. Now is the time to give serious consideration to the special niche of seasoned citizens.

How Many Are They and How Wealthy?

To carve a market niche among older Americans, it's wise to look at who they are and what their circumstances and attitudes are. This is most useful from the sale side, since most of them are looking to sell their last house. But their tastes and preferences in housing are also potentially important, since they may in fact be looking to buy for themselves, and they certainly will view prospective buyers through the prism of their own beliefs.

But don't just buy this assertion at face value. Let's look at some facts. The population of the United States will grow by about 6 percent between now and the end of the century (only five years, folks!). But the population aged 55 and older will grow by 7.5 percent, a full one-quarter faster. Moving this farther out, by the year 2010, one of every five Americans will be older than 65. See Figure 2.1. In 1994, there were 55 million Americans over the age of 55. By the turn of the century, there will be approximately 60 million. This means that the over-55s, poised to cash in on their capital gains exemption, are becoming a larger portion of our population as a whole.

More importantly, the youngest portion of that group—those between 55 and 60—will grow by 18 percent, or *three* times the national average. With the drive toward early retirement (voluntary or involuntary), some members of this group will cast their eyes on warmer, safer climates accessible to recreational activities—a natural farming target for the real estate professional.

This is an affluent group, as well. Incomes are generally high: currently, nearly 25 percent of the seasoned market consists of households earning more than $50,000 per year (the typical American family earns about $35,000). See Figure 2.2. Even as income falls, wealth continues to rise. Average household wealth for the 65-to 74-year-old group exceeds that of the 55- to 64-year-olds by about 25 percent ($100,000 v. $80,000). A great part of this net worth is home equity; 62 percent of all older Americans own their homes outright. See Figure 2.3.

The net of this is that the senior market is big enough and has enough purchasing power to command your interest.

FIGURE 2.1   Percent Distribution of the Population by Age, 1990–2010

Age	1990	1995	2000	2005	2010
Under 25	36.5	35.7	35.2	34.5	33.4
25–44	32.4	31.8	30.3	27.9	26.2
45–64	18.6	19.6	21.9	24.9	27.1
65 and over	13.7	14.2	14.2	14.4	15.0

Population Distribution by Age, 1990

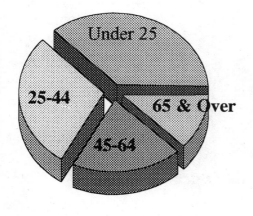

Population Distribution by Age, 2010

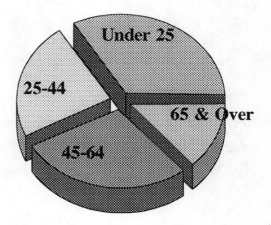

Source: U.S. Department of Commerce, Bureau of the Census.

The Reality of the Seasoned Market

Interested yet? If you are, you might want to know a bit about the tastes and habits of seasoned buyers and sellers.

1. They tend to be settled homeowners. Eight in ten own their own homes and three in four live in detached houses. Values range from about $68,000 for the over-75s to about $100,000 for the 55- to 64-year-olds. Generally, those who live in detached houses are younger, higher-income married couples.

FIGURE 2.2   Wealth Held by Older Americans

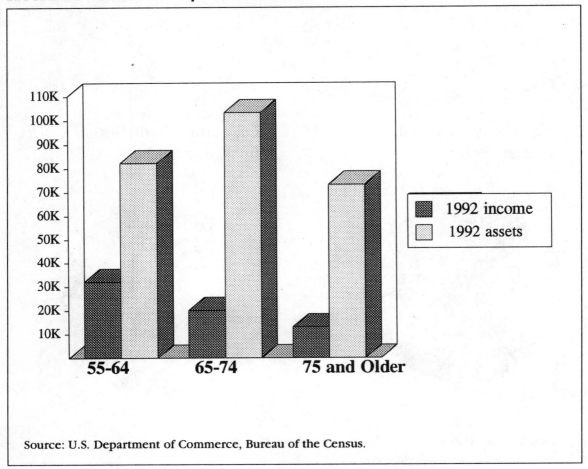

Source: U.S. Department of Commerce, Bureau of the Census.

One of the most striking characteristics of the older market is the length of tenure in their homes. More than half of homeowners aged 65 or over have lived in their current homes for over 20 years, and three out of every ten older Americans have lived in their current homes for more than 30 years. The implication here is twofold: older homeowners have considerable home equity accumulated, increasing flexibility in housing options, and they are likely to be unfamiliar with the processes of the home buying and selling market. Thus, clients in this group will need a great deal of care and handholding when they enter that market.

FIGURE 2.3   Home ownership of Older Americans

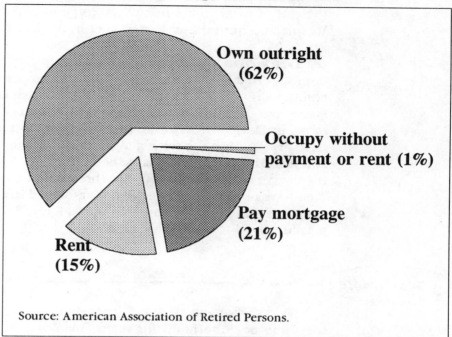

Own outright
(62%)

Occupy without
payment or rent (1%)

Pay mortgage
(21%)

Rent
(15%)

Source: American Association of Retired Persons.

Slices of Life

Nick and Marge Carstairs are fairly typical in this regard. With a six-figure income and wealth approaching seven figures, they're well off, fully aware of the world of transactions and have lived in their house for more than 20 years. Now that their family has grown and its branches have been established, they find their current home too large for their needs and requiring too much care to suit the lifestyle they want. So, it's time to move on. They have no doubts that dealing with a real estate professional is the way to go, but they've been out of the market for a long time and they're not quite certain how it's done.

People like the Carstairs offer two distinct challenges for the real estate professional. First, a great deal of education about the nature of the current housing market will be necessary to bring the buyer or seller up to date with market conditions. Second, counseling and patience are necessary as the customer moves through the raft of forms that are now an integral part of the transaction. We pick up both these themes later in the book.

2. *They don't want to move very far.* Conventional wisdom says that the retiree will follow the sun, choosing smaller accommodations near leisure activities in a warmer climate. But this is less true as time passes. Not every seasoned seller intends to move to Florida or Arizona. In fact, eight in ten older Americans have lived within the same geographic area for more than 30 years and half have been in the same house for over 30 years. Even when they move away, it's not very far: three out of four older Americans who have moved in the past five years stayed in the same state, and over half stayed in the same county. Figure 2.4 shows this trend graphically.

Slices of Life

Frank Dixon and his wife are a case in point. They've lived in the same neighborhood for many, many years. They know their neighbors, like them and in turn are liked by them. The stores and parks are all familiar. The problem now is that health problems have drastically reduced the scope of their activities. It's harder to get around and much more difficult to keep the house as nice as they'd like.

The Dixons, though, are planners and they realized that the time to move on would eventually come. But they did not migrate to the sun. Rather, with the help of real estate professionals, they relocated to a retirement community very close to their old home and neighborhood. The adjustment in their life took them from their house, but not their home.

So, don't think of the elderly market as entirely one-sided. You don't lose every seller to Arizona or Florida (and if you're doing business in the Sun Belt, don't despair: there will still be enough migration to keep those markets busy).

Nor is it only a selling market. It's true that the majority of older sellers will not buy another house when they sell their current one. But enough do to make this a two-sided market.

FIGURE 2.4   Distance of Final Move

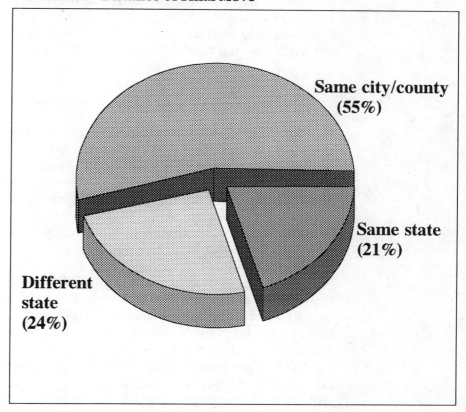

Couples like the Carstairs—the younger, more sophisticated older household—will both buy and sell and, if you can provide outstanding, sympathetic, understanding service, they'll be some of your best promoters. So the senior household niche can be a good referral market.

But, remember it's primarily a sales market, servicing the older household that needs to relocate to rental accommodations. The other aspect, relocating a household to another owned home that may be smaller, is important and may be concentrated in the same geographic area. Your older seller can easily become an older buyer as well.

3. Family is important. The most frequently mentioned reason for moving is to live closer to family. That's not unexpected, since a portion of these moves are health related. More important is the role of the family in the moving and relocation decision itself. Eight out of nine older movers consult *only* their family and friends about their living arrangements as they age.

Slices of Life

Ms. Zimmerman was an ideal client even though she was unsure of all the details of the real estate transaction. Extra care and repeated explanations were provided as part of the agent's service, and she seemed the most cooperative of sellers. That is, until a valid and lucrative offer for the property came from two women who happened to be gay. Ms. Zimmerman's disagreement with the prospective buyers' sexual orientation was so severe that she severed all contact with her agent and placed all matters in the hands of a niece.

The niece turned out to be a pivotal player. She was able to be the buffer/liaison between the aunt and the agents, and was able to explain to each the thinking behind the other's beliefs and feelings. Ultimately, she convinced her aunt that the offer was both fair and advantageous, and it was accepted.

Although the transaction finally closed, early integration of the niece into the process would have averted a great deal of heartache and clarified to the agent the full nature of the client's interests and wishes. Things like fair housing laws could have been translated to Ms. Zimmerman early in the process and thus opened a dialogue that would have unmasked attitudes that were later a barrier to the transaction.

Any real estate professional who wants to become involved in the senior market must learn to deal with not only the customer but also with the circle of family and advisers that will often provide support to the customer. Without this extended consultation, the agent will not gain the trust and respect of the seller and is unlikely to complete the transaction.

But there is an upside as well. The agent who can successfully enter the family decision process as a full participant has established a relationship with the family that may well be a source of future listings and sales. This is one of the toughest aspects of the senior market, but managing it effectively can turn that market into one of the most potentially lucrative.

In Chapter 7, we describe how the agent can (and should) create a team of his or her own to either replace or supplement the family advisers. Legal, financial and psychological talent will pay off in making the transaction work much more smoothly. The team can provide the answers that the family (particularly those that are putative heirs) needs for the comfort level to support the transaction. Besides, your team can be an effective marketing tool for establishing your reputation as a specialist in the older market.

4. They're generally unprepared to move. More than eight in ten older Americans want to stay in their current house; only 13 percent would really like to move. As a result, they don't plan: nearly a third of older Americans have not planned *at all* for their future housing needs. Even among those who anticipate moving, more than a quarter have done no planning for their housing future. See the pie chart in Figure 2.5.

Two points need to be mentioned here. First, the size of the market is still considerable even taking into account the fact that most older households don't wish to move. The 13 percent who really want to move will represent nearly 8 million households by the turn of the century. That is a considerable pool that gets bigger when those who don't anticipate moving eventually do become movers.

The second point deals with an expanded role for the real estate professional. The best entry point to the older market may well be in the area of counseling. The lack of planning on the part of the older household means that a knowledgeable professional who presents an understandable picture of future possibilities is an attractive partner to the older American.

Despite thorough preparation and the assistance of a close relative, the move of Alice Thornton was very difficult. Seemingly, she was all prepared to relocate from a house to a condominium near her son, but no unit seemed to be right. In reality, there was nothing wrong with the accommodations—Alice had just made no commitment in her own heart and mind to move.

FIGURE 2.5   **Planning for Future Housing Needs**

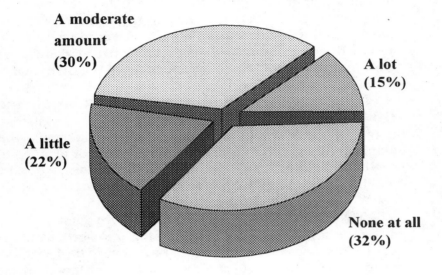

How much have you planned for your future housing needs?

A moderate amount (30%)

A lot (15%)

A little (22%)

None at all (32%)

Source: American Association of Retired Persons.

⬭ *Slices of Life* ▷────────────────────────────

    Without the internal psychological buy-in, the decision could not be made. In the end, the move was made, but even now Alice complains about overlooking the dumpster . . . which is true, if you lean out over the balcony and crane your neck real hard.

    If you look down the line at the population statistics, there may be a business investment here. Counseling homesellers—regardless of age—about how to plan for the long term will be an increasing need. You can do this either alone or by putting together a team. Moreover, real estate agents have an advantage over financial planners in that their relationships with households are richer and cover a wider range of family needs and events.

5. *They live alone and like it.* More than a third of older Americans live alone, and, more surprisingly, nearly half would like to live alone. When they are not alone, the vast majority live with spouses or children. Even so, when they have a choice of where to live, older Americans will congregate with people of their own age and interests. Generally, seasoned households view their peers as friendlier and more helpful than households of other ages.

This only reinforces the reliant nature of many older households. Because they live alone, older households tend to build protective cocoons about themselves, usually using friends and family. Becoming part of this cocoon is difficult and may require earning the trust of several members of the extended household. But, once involved, the ability to serve as the family adviser is magnified.

6. *Peace and quiet is a major neighborhood attraction.* In defiance of conventional wisdom, older Americans value a peaceful environment and the proximity of people with common interests far more than they fear for their safety and security. This is particularly true of homeowners, and especially the older households with relatively high incomes. In fact, more than half of all over-55s feel very secure in their homes, and only a third are very concerned about their future security. While these numbers are pushed up by retirement community dwellers, even the majority of city dwellers considered themselves secure.

This attitude will affect the manner in which the real estate professional approaches an older seller with a potential buyer. The older homeowner is concerned not only about the value of the property, but also about the neighborhood. They will be reluctant to introduce elements into the community that they perceive may negatively affect its peacefulness. This perception can apply to anyone from simply younger households with children to people who are "not like us," as was the case with Ms. Zimmerman.

The real estate professional walks a real tightrope here. Fair housing laws preclude any discrimination that may result from an older household's attempt to retain the character of the neighborhood for the benefit of those staying behind. You need to know them, and we deal with this topic extensively in Chapter 8.

But, quite frankly, for most older sellers neighbors count more than any law on the books. So the seller will often persist in this presumption, to the detriment of the business relationship. Once again, the successful transaction requires more work and care than is usual.

7. *Physical and fiscal health dominate the future.*
The primary concerns of older Americans, by far, are failing health and dwindling wealth. As you might guess, the wealthier worry more about health and the poorer care more about wealth. Many are like the Dixons in that health has forced them to move, but unlike them in that they haven't thought about the "how." Those that have considered the possible need to move most likely have saved for the future or reduced their living expenses. Only a quarter have created either financial or health care powers of attorney with a family member, friend or adviser.

Once again, this points to the need for the team and the expansion of activity beyond real estate services. The creation of a planning team that offers legal, relocation and financial planning advice as well as real estate services provides one-stop shopping that will create value for the senior household.

8. *Living costs are getting higher and less controllable.*
Over the past several years, major increases in housing costs have come in the form of utility bills and property taxes. This is no less true for older Americans who face an additional burden of fixed or declining incomes. In fact, concern over both areas has increased dramatically to the point that more than eight of ten older Americans are concerned about future increases in living costs generated by property taxes and three in four are concerned about utility cost increases. See Figure 2.6.

The opportunity for real estate professionals here is twofold. First, they can be a source of information about financial relief available to older homeowners faced with escalating utility and property tax burdens. This will cause the older household to look to the professional as an asset and help solidify the trust relationship that is a prerequisite to doing business in the older market.

FIGURE 2.6   Concerns about Future Increased Costs

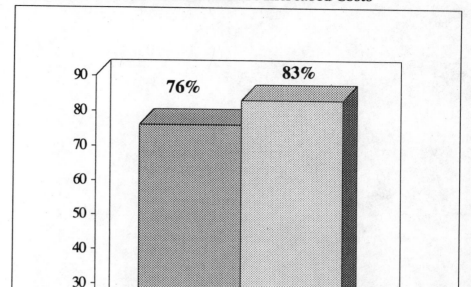

Second, the prospect of higher taxes and utility costs when set against the housing alternatives that may be available can help the older household get over the threshold decision of relocating. It is thus integral to helping the older household work through a planning process.

Chapter 3

Winning Credibility with Compassion

Slices of Life

Diane Wilson was referred to her REALTOR® by past clients. She and her 40-year-old son were living together in a large house that had been home to their family for 35 years. Her husband had died five years earlier, and maintaining the house eventually became too much for Ms. Wilson and her son. She decided to locate in a neighboring state where she had some friends and her son had some business opportunities.

Before they could make the move, the old house had to be brought up to date so that it could be sold. The house was structurally sound and very large, but showed some obsolescence. On top of that, the real estate market was suffering from a weak local economy. Thus, the problems on the selling side were twofold: preparing the property and pricing it correctly in a down market.

The agents advised the Wilsons to concentrate on the sale of the old house, since this would be where the most work was to be done. If that could be accomplished first, relocation matters could be considered with little or no stress. Relocating first would only place them far away from the problems of renovation and pricing.

Getting an offer on the house took 18 months, but the Wilsons were ready to get to work on relocation immediately. Although well into her seventies, Ms. Wilson was mentally sharp. Still, she delegated her son (who was also her close adviser) to be the buffer, translator and conduit between her and the REALTOR®. This necessitated forging two relationships.

While showing properties to Ms. Wilson and her son, the REALTOR® uncovered several concerns that Ms. Wilson had as to type of house, neighborhood, future marketability and a host of other areas. Specifically, she worried about her future ability to handle steps and so wanted a single-level home; she wanted a quiet neighborhood; she was concerned about her son's ability to handle the finances of a house in the event that she died, and so needed a home that he could sell and use the proceeds to move into smaller quarters. Eventually, the agents found the house the Wilsons wanted. The whole process turned out to be a win-win: the clients found the house that exactly met their unique needs. But every client has unique needs; it's just that older customers may have a longer list and may be less forthcoming about expressing them.

When you consider all the statistics and analyze case studies like that of the Wilsons, a simple rule emerges: to deal effectively in the older market, several qualities are of crucial importance.

Trust. All forward momentum begins here. Without the creation of an adequate level of trust between the agent and seller, the transaction is doomed. Oh, you may get to closing, but the failure to gain the seller's *complete* trust will far more often than not eliminate all referrals and any future business.

Without an adequate level of trust, the emotional toll on both seller and practitioner will be devastating. The building of a strong relationship with seasoned citizens often begins with a family member or an unrelated, but trusted, third party (e.g., an attorney or a physician). Your ability to capture the confidence of that individual will pave the way for your relationship with the seller.

Slices of Life

Nick Carstairs has been a lucrative source of business for his real estate agent. His transactions alone generated over $24,000 in commission income in 14 months, and that doesn't count referrals . . . and he's not done yet. None of this would have materialized if the REALTOR® had not established a solid reputation in the community and had not won Nick's trust at the outset of their relationship.

You need to anticipate involving the third party early on when you sense that the seller may not be completely comfortable with or fully capable of handling the decisions required to complete the sale. Trust must precede, and prevail throughout, your relationship with the seller.

Patience. More than any other skill, patience may be the requisite for sustained success in this specialty. Your seller may well have been out of the buying and selling loop for a number of years. The average tenure for the over-65 homeowner exceeds 20 years, which is several generations in the real estate business. These sellers need time to understand current market practice.

Slices of Life

Carol Mayne never expected to be in the real estate process. Oh, she knew that she would be relocating because of retirement, but the sudden death of her husband thrust her into a decision-making world about which she knew nothing. Her husband had handled all financial matters, and Mrs. Mayne was utterly unprepared to act as decision maker in a real estate transaction. She was able to do so in part because of a solid support group—her family—but also because her agent took the time to explain and re-explain what would be happening and what she needed to do.

The listing process may take three or four visits (rather than the typical two) over an extended period of time, with the pace being set by the seller. (This is detailed in Chapter 5.) Again, include all trusted parties early on.

Throughout the relationship and the transaction, you must expect to be constantly and readily accessible. The ability to consistently meet such expectations can be burdensome and perhaps unrealistic for even the best of salespeople. Patience is a prime ingredient in the formula for success: if you don't have it, consider using a partner or assistant who does.

Empathy. The quality of empathy is a sister to the resource of patience in building and maintaining solid relationships with older households. Remember, your clients are making really big life decisions. In many cases, they are proceeding from a feeling of inevitability, or in a time of grief and travail, or because of pressure from relatives, but not through an entirely rational process. Figure out from the beginning whether a given move is viewed by the seller with fear or expectation or, more likely, a mixture of positives and negatives.

As you might guess, ambiguity goes with the territory. You may be called upon to help in the decision-making process, sort of prelisting counseling. This involves working to understand the life situation of the sellers and the degree of their resolve before the technical aspects of the selling process can be initiated. You must also recognize situations when the best service you can perform is to advise the client *not* to sell.

Because moving is such a difficult decision, reassuring and reaffirming the sellers (and/or their families) that the decision is a good one will be an ongoing task. Learn to expect a certain degree of backsliding with regard to commitment to the move and be prepared to respond sensitively. You must recognize this ambivalence about the decision to move in the uncooperative behavior or unrealistic expectations you will encounter. The agent must be empathic to the barriers created by both the seller's circumstances and the selling process.

Education. Educating the seller throughout the process is a given in every real estate transaction, but especially so when the client is an older household. The details of transferring property have multiplied geometrically in recent years. The proliferation of forms and the legal and regulatory framework that control the transfer of housing necessitate thoughtful planning and presentation of information in a user friendly manner at appropriate points in the course of the transaction. Information about the process and what to expect must be reviewed and then reintroduced and reinforced in manageable bites.

A printed guide that the seller can refer to periodically will save a great deal of time. This can be prepared easily by cataloging your experiences over several transactions and using these as the basis for the seller's companion piece. Examples of this can be found in Chapter 12.

Beyond this, the relative inexperience of the seller may necessitate confirming conversations in writing. This will save you time and emotional energy. Finally, take the time to ask "Do you understand?" and "Do you have any questions?"

Expertise. Here being an expert goes beyond knowledge directly related to the real estate transaction. It includes being a source of information about the resources that these sellers may need in order to proceed to settlement. Giving the seller access to these support resources provides the added benefit of assigning burdens that might otherwise fall to the agent. Developing and updating these sources of support is especially valuable. Again, please refer to Chapter 12 for detailed examples.

The remaining chapters of the book provide a step-by-step approach to dealing with the practicalities of serving the aging market, including the resources you can use both to identify buyers and gather listings, and to use in supporting your clients' transaction process.

One final word. After reading these three chapters, you may be struck by the difficulty of establishing and maintaining a business niche in this area. For a certain segment—primarily the oldest, the frailest and the poorest—this is true.

But like any demographic group, the over-55s are rich in diversity. A large portion of them will have full control over their affairs: they've planned carefully, saved diligently and done their homework. Their work experience has predisposed them to value delegation to qualified professionals. These households will almost be easier to deal with than any other part of the housing market, if the proper understanding and empathy are applied. And their numbers are exploding!

So, look hard at the opportunities from our aging population. We think it will serve you very well.

Chapter 4

Understanding the Way It Was

Let's face it, times have certainly changed over the last 30 years. In fact, they have changed over the last 30 minutes. Working with people who may not have purchased or sold a home over those 30 years virtually guarantees a certain amount of confusion and uncertainty. For the older buyer and seller, it is sometimes frightening to try to comprehend the changes that have occurred in the way property is transferred. Complicated lists of documents must be sifted through. In all likelihood a number of total strangers will be involved with the buyer or seller to see the transaction through to a successful conclusion and those strangers become privy to people's personal lives.

More People, More Paper

Above and beyond the sheer volume of transaction documents required of buyers and sellers today is the significance and relative novelty, at least to older households, of the issues addressed in many of those documents. Issues related to fair housing, agency and disclosure are enormously significant in terms of creating potential liability for buyer, seller and agent. Most of the time, the client has little appreciation of their importance, particularly in the areas of fair housing and agency. We know that the reader appreciates their importance.

Consider, though, the Geeres, who decided to sell their home so that they could enjoy their golden years in a physically and financially more manageable home, have the extra money to travel and still have a buffer in case of an emergency. They would go on to purchase an attractive home in a safe setting that allowed them to meet all their goals, but both sides of this transaction were overwhelming to these people who hadn't been in the housing market for better than 30 years.

"When we bought our last house in the late 1950s, it was simple. The REALTOR® met us at our hotel and proceeded to show us a number of houses that he felt would interest us. After looking at eight houses, my wife and I settled for a cozy Cape Cod on a tree-lined street surrounded by a white picket fence. The house was our vision of charm and seemed to call to us to move in. We decided right then and there that this was the house of our dreams, so we instructed our REALTOR® to draw up the papers. This was done on a one-page form with a check for one hundred dollars. Within three hours, the property was ours."

When asked what happened next, he replied, "Our REALTOR® walked us down to the local bank, introduced us to the banker, explained that we were moving in to work for the DuPont Company and that we needed a loan to purchase the house we just bought. We filled out two forms and were told that we would have an answer within the next few days. Sure enough, we got our loan just 48 hours after walking into the bank and were well on our way."

"The closing could not have gone more smoothly. The lawyer who compiled the paperwork and deed had us in and out within 30 minutes and had us sign our names a total of five times. From that point on and for over 30 years we had a place we called home."

The Geeres never gave a serious second thought to obtaining their mortgage. After all, they had completed the necessary paperwork and Mr. Geere was starting his new job in the next week. There was no doubt that they would receive their loan. The buyers probably visited the sellers on one or more occasions just to get to know them. Perhaps the sellers shared a few fond memories that had taken place in the house that was to become the Geeres' new home. No doubt the home's quirks and idiosyncrasies were explained, too.

As often as not the buyer and seller relationship went beyond a business transaction. They found themselves dealing with one another as new acquaintances or even friends. Buying, and selling, a home was by its nature a pleasant experience.

That was then. This is now.

When purchasing their new, scaled-down home, the Geeres submitted an offer on an eight-page document that was as cumbersome as it was long. The offer was countered twice before being accepted and had a number of conditions to be met including a home inspection contingency, a radon contingency, a seller's property disclosure form (to be signed by all parties), an agency disclosure form, a home warranty form, a business relationship form and an interest bearing account form. A few other miscellaneous documents completed the homebuyer's package. In total, the Geeres signed more paperwork just to place an offer than they did 30 years ago to complete the entire process.

After the initial round of paperwork was completed and the sellers had "accepted" the offer, the home inspection loomed on the horizon. The Geeres, while appreciative of their agent's recommendation and explanation, couldn't help but feel apprehensive about the impending inspection. They felt that they were unduly invading the sellers' privacy, that the request for an inspection signaled their distrust of the sellers and they were uneasy about what flaws might be revealed in the course of the inspection. "It's all so formal," they lamented. "Have things changed so much over just three decades?" Well, yes, from a legal perspective, they certainly have.

The home inspector checked everything in his three-hour tour. He even dismantled the heater and removed the cover on the electrical box to make sure that everything was in order. From the top of the roof to the corners of the crawl space, not an inch was left unsurveyed. The inspector offered a list of items that might need attention in the next several years. The inspection, although stressful, proved to be helpful to all parties concerned. The anticipation of problems caused a reaction at first, but fears were laid to rest upon the completion of the inspection.

The Geeres were then introduced to another new concern of the 1990s—radon. Their REALTOR® had to explain what it was, and how it could affect them in the new home. Picocuries per liter, remediation, radon warning levels and venting systems were all terms new to them. They needed to understand the potential impact of the gas in the event that it was found in the house and exceeded

Environmental Protection Agency (EPA) standards. They had to sign a release verifying their understanding.

Next came mortgage preparation, not to be confused with mortgage application. First, there was the form explaining items needed for a mortgage application. This list of over 30 items was just the tip of the iceberg. As if that weren't enough, they were given a lengthy list of mortgage companies that, on the surface, looked very much alike. Upon closer inspection, however, each company offered numerous products ranging from the traditional 30-year fixed-rate mortgage, with points of course ("What's a point?" they asked. "Is this something new?") to adjustable-rate mortgages, buy-downs, balloons, etc., etc., etc. The fact is, the Geeres were so unprepared for the maze that is the mortgage process that they had no idea what was in store for them. At one point they contemplated paying cash to avoid the scrutiny imposed by everyone involved in the purchase. With patience and persistence, they made their way through the confusing jungle of procedures and redundancy. (Wait until they hear about computer loan origination or CLO's.)

They proceeded to closing. "This should be simple enough, right?" Right. At the settlement table, the Geeres signed their name a total of 34 times but ended up owning the new house after just one and one half hours.

What makes this story so striking as we transfer real estate in the 1990s is the sheer simplicity of the transaction. The actual acquisition of a home today doesn't differ much procedurally from the acquisition 30 years ago. The dramatic difference lies in the number of people involved in the transaction and the emergence of related variables. Then there were a REALTOR®, a banker, a buyer, a seller and an attorney. Naturally there was less formality. There were fewer parties and there was less information to be exchanged.

The most obvious differences have to be the number of people involved and the formality of the process. Of course the primary players are still in the picture: REALTOR®, seller, buyer and attorney, but who are all these other people and what are they doing here? Our poor sellers and buyers need a ledger to keep them straight. "The bank" has been replaced by banks and there are other lenders, too. Financing options are offered in every flavor by mortgage brokers. The banker is now more often than not an originator who is followed by a mortgage processor and then by a representative from the lender's closing department. There was a home inspector and a radon inspector. Let us not forget the attorney (or title clerk), the settlement secretary, the appraiser or the termite inspector either. Lots of people doing a lot of different things.

And Now, Let's Talk Money

The mortgage process itself ranks high on the list of stress builders. The documents, documentation and explanations create a long and winding trail—of paper, that is. There are verifications, authorizations and disclosures to be waded through. There are notifications to be read and signed, such as the HUD notice regarding lead paint. Employment verifications depend upon employers and their human resources departments for completion and timely return. Savings accounts must be scrutinized and deposits and withdrawals substantiated. Other sources of funds are equally prone to probes. How about those credit checks? At least the Geeres weren't cursed with a common name like Jones! Receipt of the Federal Truth-in-Lending statement is guaranteed to generate an eye-popping reaction if it is not clearly explained beforehand. Even the most sophisticated buyers struggle to grasp the purpose of some of the documents that they are asked to sign.

Is it any wonder that for days after the final decision on a lender is reached and the application process initiated our buyers are still reeling from the experience? Unfortunately, it may not become any easier as the process wears on, especially for those who are unaccustomed to the demands of the circumstances. Read on.

The next step in the mortgage application process is the packaging of the loan information in a way that will make it acceptable for purchase in the secondary mortgage market. Loan packagers have a significant responsibility for the final approval of the loan. The cast here consists of the originator, whom the buyer has met by this time, the processor, who assembles various exhibits for presentation at the next level, the appraiser, who is hired to independently confirm that the property holds value equal to or greater than the loan amount and the underwriter(s), responsible for lining up investors to fund the loan and assuring that the loan can be sold to the secondary mortgage market. The underwriter, though never seen by the borrower, will make the ultimate decision to approve the loan or not.

Communication among the various members of this team is essential for obtaining a timely mortgage approval.

The way mortgages were handled 30 years ago was certainly different from the process now. In fact, changes are coming so rapidly that the process may change from one 30-day period to the next. REALTORS® have a hard time keeping up with new conditions and requirements, so doesn't it stand to reason that the public, particularly those who haven't been in the marketplace for a number of years, would be confused?

Where the Agent Comes In

Our job as real estate professionals is to help clarify and simplify the process. And it stands to reason that the longer our client has been removed from the scene, the more explaining we may have to do. The Geeres are typical buyers in that they required considerable education about new developments in the real estate industry. The examples described are but a few facing buyers in the 1990s. Many other situations arise during a transaction, some as a matter of the contract and others not anticipated.

The best way to avoid continual crisis intervention is to anticipate and plan for events to come. By preparing buyers ahead of time through written and oral explanations and being ready to address the unexpected, the agent is doing what comes necessarily if not naturally. Some might argue that this aspect of our job is the most valuable service rendered and ultimately makes the difference between a satisfying and a simply satisfactory sale. The smart agent will stay on top of new information dealing with issues such as radon, home inspections, mortgage changes and the like so that his or her clients can be best informed.

When working with these buyers and sellers, think about how it was when they were in the market in the 1960s, 1950s or even earlier. Empathize with them and provide the resources they need to successfully negotiate the sales process today. As you empower them they will teach you. Both you and your future clients will benefit from the insights you gain. Thoughtful questions posed by clients intent upon understanding exactly what is going on and its significance have helped us to smooth the path for many who will follow in their footsteps. Your value as a resource will enable you to retain clients and customers for life.

Chapter 5

Considerations When Listing with the Seasoned Citizen

Success in serving the senior market lies in recognizing two things. The first is that no matter how much time and paperwork sophisticated technology can save, older Americans demand access to and attention from their sales agent or representative. Time-saving techniques are not well appreciated by these clients. They grew up in a simpler world and it can be difficult for them to fall into step with the new one. But you can view this as an ideal marriage of people and information. Use all the technology at your disposal to prepare and execute the transaction, but make the technology invisible to the client.

Second, the selling process is far too complicated and information-rich to explain fully in one or two visits. You will have to deliver more information in smaller bites. Information to which the seller is entitled and for which the agent is legally responsible must be provided in manageable amounts at appropriate times, repeated frequently and probably backed up through the use of checklists and printed material.

Keeping these two guidelines in mind as you proceed will pay off in smoother, more successful transactions, and the preparation undertaken for this part of the market will transfer effectively to other market segments as well. Throughout this chapter you'll find suggestions and recommendations to help you make highest and best use of your time while satisfying the sometimes special needs of older sellers and buyers.

Establishing the Relationship with a Senior Client

From the first point of contact, begin asking yourself and others, depending upon their availability, a series of questions like the following:

- Does the seller seem secure in the decision to sell?
- Does the seller indicate that family members are involved or available to help with the move?
- Does the prospective client seem to understand the things that you are talking about?
- Does the seller seem cooperative?
- How does the person or couple seem to feel about making this move?
- Do they seem in control of details associated with the physical move?

It may take more than one contact to answer these questions, but the answers are vitally important in determining how much and what kinds of support resources you will need, so keep them in mind from your first introduction to the prospect or his or her representative. Let's take a closer look at this first point of contact.

The Initial Contact

This is the first opportunity to gain a basic picture of the prospective seller. How did this person come to you? Who made the first contact? The seller? A family member? An attorney or another representative on the seller's behalf? That in itself may tell a lot about who your primary contact will be and about the nature of the ensuing move.

It is also useful to understand the context of the move. Question the party briefly about the circumstances surrounding the move, the time line anticipated and the general profile of the home to be sold. Obviously, the more information you can gather at this point, the more you know about what to expect in the subsequent face-to-face visit and the more time you'll have to accomplish other things at that time.

Now let's go through the sequence of activities that will conclude with the sale of the home.

The First Visit: Explaining the Initial Steps

You want to walk away from this visit with enough information to complete a market analysis of the property. For most listings this will be a short, fact-finding visit of 30 to 45 minutes. This meeting with the senior client and his or her trusted advisers is crucial for establishing rapport and beginning to build the foundation of trust. Remember, you are dealing with a dwelling made not just of bricks and mortar but of memories, and years of family life are threaded throughout. You may find yourself in an extremely confidential position. You may be the first person outside the family to learn of the decision to move. The seller may be articulating for the first time the reasons leading up to the decision.

There is much to be accomplished in this visit and much to be learned. Be sure to provide full information about yourself and your company, and convey it by both manner and spoken word. Give an overview of what will happen between the first and second visits and some of the other details to expect. Seriously consider introducing written detail about "next steps" in the selling process and the importance of proper pricing. Make sure the seller understands that you need him or her to read the material before your next visit.

The Second Visit: The Right Price and Other Matters

The primary goals of this meeting are to arrive at an acceptable listing price and see that the condition of the home will enhance salability. Of course, in order to reach those goals you must first review the market analysis and pricing recommendations, determine if the seller is willing and/or able to undertake work on the home to enhance its marketability, then reach agreement on the listing price, review and complete the listing agreement and related documents and go over the various selling expenses. That completed, you'll want to generally outline the steps in the selling process so that the seller knows what to expect. Oh yes, let's not forget that this meeting should also serve to cement the relationship between you and your seller.

Under the best of conditions that's a lot of ground to cover. Some practitioners would argue that this is *the* most important meeting you will have with any seller in the course of your relationship. Why? Because all the effort spent trying to market an overpriced home will not accomplish the goal of selling it. Proper pricing is the primary objective of this meeting and, ideally, this is your opportunity to prepare the seller for the offer that will follow. The nature of the individual seller will determine the pace of the meeting and how many of the objectives can be achieved.

Let's zero in on the pricing issue. As is the case in every other successful listing appointment, *you've got to be prepared.* Some sellers may live in dated homes, out of touch with the realities of the marketplace, reluctant to hear what you have to say and unwilling to accept your conclusions. Most will have only one or more of these characteristics. Nonetheless, remember: don't prepare and you have no prayer!

In fairness to both the seller and the agent, the presentation must be logically and clearly organized, and the data in place to explain and justify recommendations. Proceeding in this manner builds your case by allowing the sellers to see how you reach the conclusions about the market and pricing and gives them the chance to ask questions. At the finish, most sellers (most of the time) will concur with your conclusions and accept your advice.

Substantiating your conclusions through the use of a simple, straightforward printed report not only lends credibility through the medium, but also provides the seller, and any trusted others involved, with a tangible reference for further consideration. This information is greatly appreciated by most sellers and may come in handy as a point of reference if a price reduction is necessary or an offer needs to be put in proper perspective.

A further thought on preparing printed material. Be sure that everything you plan to present is meaningful to the recipient and is written in language geared to the layperson, with content clearly stated. Consider the size of the print and graphics on the page. Few will find slightly larger print a negative and many will be grateful for the consideration. In all of your dealings with clients in this group (or for that matter all buyers and sellers) don't talk down to them, but make sure that the communication is clear. Even the most sophisticated of sellers will appreciate your efforts.

Back to events unfolding at the kitchen table . . . .

If the sellers do not agree with your pricing recommendations, your next steps will depend on the reason for their disagreement. Either they understand fully what you have shared with them and simply do not want to accept the conclusions, or they genuinely believe that based upon their own criteria their home has a value greater than your market analysis supports.

In the case of a seller who understands but does not accept, patience, persistence and perhaps a limited testing of the market may still permit accurate pricing and a successfully concluded sale. However, in the event that the seller cannot accept the basis for your conclusions, then this may not be a viable listing. To break the deadlock, especially for an unusual home, consider having a fee-based appraisal done.

Your decision to decline to list an unsalable property is a good one for your business and is also in the best interests of the seller. An overpriced listing sitting on the market, unshown and unsold, is no service to the seller. Though there will always be an agent willing to accept the overpriced home, you have done your part to educate and ensure that the sellers do not make that choice out of ignorance. (And this little explanation offered to certain reluctant sellers can be powerfully persuasive.)

This counsel is especially important with senior sellers because the proceeds of this sale may be the lion's share of their future financial resources. That need, in conjunction with ignorance about real estate values, may create unrealistic expectations. They may also believe that regardless of list price an interested buyer will make an offer. It is incumbent upon you to clarify such misconceptions.

Considering the Home's Condition

Of course, any pricing discussion must address the condition of the home. The discussion should lead to the subject of preparations required to ready the home for the market. Consider the challenges you face in addressing this subject:

- In many cases your first challenge lies in helping the seller to understand what defines condition and how good or improved condition may not necessarily mean a higher price for the property, but simply decrease the time on the market and contribute to getting the job done. That's a big one!
- Statistics show that older households are more likely to have lived in the home for a long time. A treasured accumulation of lifetime memories to the seller may just appear as clutter to prospective buyers. That stockpile of possessions now meets the moment of reckoning. Like most of us, it's no

easier for seniors to face those big and little decisions now than it has been each and every day of their lives.

- Sometimes, the actual owner of the home is unable or unavailable to help in the purging process. Those charged with the disposition of the property may not be interested or readily available either.
- The decor may have grown old with the owner. Having lived with them for 20 or 30 years, the seller may not realize that purple and pink walls and turquoise appliances diminish the sale value of the house.
- Some older sellers may be particularly sensitive to your recommendations, easily offended or insulted by your suggestions. Reactions like these must be seen in the larger context of the move at hand and the emotional trauma of uprooting a lifetime of living.
- Some sellers in this stage of their lives may understand the benefits of a house in good condition but are unable or disinclined to undertake the efforts to meet the time line.

Again, as in preparing to market any salable listing, the agent needs to assess the situation and prioritize the work that needs to be completed. The job is simpler if the actual occupant of the home has already moved or the sellers' circumstances permit them the option of moving out before the house is placed for sale. Not only is it easier to market the house empty, but the agent has more latitude in directing the work to be done. Getting rid of everything is often an easier decision than getting rid of some things.

Other members of the support team discussed in Chapter 7 can be especially helpful in this arena. Family members or trusted friends can be called upon to reinforce the recommendations that you have made, help to implement them or take care of the work.

In arranging for renovations of the home, you have a great advantage in your ability to serve as a referral source/coordinator of service providers. One of the greatest services that you bring to the client is your knowledge of those tradespeople and community resources available to make the repairs and remove the belongings, coordinate the move and clean up along the way. But agents should avoid taking direct responsibility for the choice of provider or assuming personal responsibility for work. Let the seller know who is available, reliable and well recommended. *Your reputation and legal liability require that you keep an arm's length from the final selection of tradespeople.* It is always good business practice to offer more than one name and to document your involvement.

Empty or occupied, the first order of business is the curb appeal of the property, followed closely by the degree of crowding, clutter and cleanliness. Start with a basic assessment of the age and condition of systems. These will show up in your representations, but a seller's disclosure form may prove attractive to potential buyers. As of August 1994, these forms are mandatory in 25 states. They have gone far to reduce agent/broker liability and are widely accepted by both buyers and sellers.

Most of the time your inspection and the owner's records will provide adequate historical detail. When the owner can't help with this information it may be wise to recommend a prelisting home inspection, especially when the systems appear dated or in disrepair. Suspicious conditions or obvious problems may require the opinion of a subcontractor or repair specialist followed by a decision to repair.

Sometimes, when faced with a faded beauty or worse and sellers who are not receptive to guidance in this area, the agent has no choice but to factor the deferred maintenance, functional obsolescence and/or dated decorating into the offering price. There's no reason to feel bad about it. Just like the market, it is what it is and we just have to work with it!

When you and the seller have agreed on price, try to provide as complete an estimate as possible of the seller's closing costs. This is another important aspect of this meeting for several reasons:

1. You're telling the seller his or her bottom line. Ultimately sellers are less interested in the listing or sale price of their home than they are in the net figure after all charges are tallied. This information may play a big part in their moving plans.

2. You're eliminating a surprise. Surprises relating to the pocketbook are not welcome, particularly to older households. Use this opportunity to continue educating the seller about the costs related to the sale of the property. But emphasize that this figure is an estimate at this time, why it must be so and that it will be revised and fine-tuned as the final closing date approaches.

Getting the Listing: A Lot of Paper

Now that you've determined an accurate price, the last major hurdle to cross lies in the completion of paperwork necessary to list the home. The ever-broadening scope of subjects that have become a part of the real estate sales process and accompanying proliferation of documentation can contribute significantly to seller stress—and agent stress too, for that matter.

It's not so much that the individual components are beyond the comprehension of the average layperson, but there are just so many components. Factor in the use of legal terms and there is some serious sorting out to be done. This is even more complicated with senior households for whom much of this paper was unnecessary when they were last in the market. But even so, we must accommodate our business practices to incorporate not only the medium but more importantly, the *message*. In today's world it will not suffice to direct the client to the bottom of the page and say, "Sign here." No matter how detailed or encompassing the documents with which you work, you must assume responsibility for conveying the information contained in them and ensuring that the sellers understand it. That's an awesome responsibility in the best of circumstances and these aren't always the best of circumstances.

Begin by knowing your audience and arranging to have the older seller's circle of trust and your support team on hand for this review and signing. But don't invite the whole town. While one additional person is usually an asset, more than that can necessitate group consensus, which becomes time-consuming and even more confusing to all involved. Your judgment and ability to control the meeting is required.

Whether you have the seller read the documents and ask questions, or you read them aloud, consider providing an oral summary of the items covered. The choice depends upon you and the person with whom you are working. We have all been in situations where we knew that the client did not really understand what he or she was reading or even our explanation. That's not a good feeling for either party. If you sense that this is the case and there is no member of the support team present, suggest having one of them review the paperwork.

It makes sense to think through the key points of each form and be prepared to cover those in more depth and/or reduce them to written notes to be given to the seller. Be on the lookout for terms that may not be understood and consciously avoid acronyms and real estate jargon. Look to emphasize items and issues that consistently come up after the listing agreement is signed, but over the course of the listing period. Enlarge the print on all forms.

Much of this is common sense and applies equally to the agreement of sale to follow.

When the pricing and listing agenda is complete, the next step is to come to a clear understanding about showing procedures and guidelines for the showing of the property, what to expect in terms of showing activity, how and when you will be communicating with the seller and what to expect by way of marketing activities over the coming weeks. These understandings are best reinforced through the written word—that is, a ledger for keeping a running log of appointments made, a calendar of marketing events, etc.

Coaching homeowners in best behavior during showings is a perfect example of the need to guide and prepare them for the realities of home selling. Eager, well intentioned sellers often feel that they need to personally conduct a tour of their home for the REALTOR® and customers (the guests). The resulting discomfort and pressure brought to bear on the prospective buyers, of course, creates a negative effect. Tactfully explain that though the REALTOR® may not know the features of the home as well as the homeowner, he or she does know the personality and the needs of the customer. While it is not necessary to leave the home while it's being shown, best behavior calls for giving the lookers space and being available for questions. Chapter 12 offers detailed handouts regarding showings.

If it seems that you've covered an incredible amount of ground at this point, you have. Imagine how shell-shocked sellers feel at this stage of the game. If you've done your job well to this point, however, the hardest part is done, no matter what may lie ahead.

Chapter 6

Navigating the Road to Sold

Seasoned sellers need to know what to expect around the next bend on the road to sold. They want and deserve to know what's going to happen tomorrow, next week and next month. The efforts that you've made to build your case and win their trust will now be put to further tests. When you depart with the signed listing agreement in hand, you leave behind someone who may still be wondering, "Did I list my home with the right person?" and "Will they do what they promised to do?" Whether or not your seller is able or inclined to ask these questions, we are obligated to answer them by our actions.

Preparing the Seller for What To Expect

Remember the advice about giving information in small bites at appropriate times? Providing a marketing plan at the outset of the listing period is a good way to keep the seller in the loop and offers accountability at the same time. The degree of detail that you provide depends upon how willing you are to open your marketing activities to scrutiny. Of course it is always better to promise less and deliver more rather than the other way around. This is especially so with the senior seller, who may have more interest in the accountability aspect than would others with less time for such tracking. In any case, specific plans of action are increasingly expected of us to demonstrate proactivity and advocacy for our clients.

Many sales agents make it a practice to give their sellers support materials that explain what to expect and what is expected of them. Storing this kind of information in a computer enables the agent to tailor it to a particular seller, emphasizing those points that are most important in a given situation. You may decide that certain sellers require a softer tone or that a particular subject is better handled in a face-to-face conversation. Computer-generated materials give you that flexibility. Another good handout that anticipates the offer to purchase might include a glossary of real estate terms and explanations of inspections associated with the sale of property.

Maintaining predictable communication is another means to reassure the sellers that you're very much in the picture if not necessarily in their living rooms. Plans for phone communication should be established early on and honored faithfully. In addition to calls that you commit to make weekly or following a showing, you need to allow ample latitude for the seller's calls to you. It has been our experience—and our mothers concurred—that as people grow older they are increasingly prone to focus on small details, feel a strong need to address any and all issues right now and expect immediate access to us and immediate resolution of the concern. Although we can appreciate the reasons behind the behavior, the challenge is to avoid being on-call 24 hours a day while assuring the seller that the issue will be handled in a timely fashion. This isn't always easy to do. Tactfully advising them of how and when you can be reached and reassuring them that you are in control of the situation may help you to hold onto a bit more of your private life.

A few words about house calls: the seller's personality and your sense of his or her comfort level as determined by phone communication will dictate how often it will be necessary to sit down face-to-face. If a rule of thumb says you see most of your sellers once a month or so, consider that these homesellers may appreciate the reassurance of a visit every couple of weeks. Often the length of the visit or meeting is less important than the frequency.

Other printed communications are beneficial, too. Things such as copies of ads run and reports on the frequency of calls received about the home and other items that can be easily generated are usually welcomed by these sellers. Producing these reports need not take a lot of your time either. After a predetermined period, usually 30 to 45 days, it should be time for a status report. Composite information about the showings to date, comparable homes that have been listed for sale and sold in the time period and other comments on the market should be shared with the seller. While the report may be sent, it should be preceded or followed by a phone call or visit.

Prepare Your Sellers for the Offer

Along the way it's wise to prepare the seller for the offer to come. This can be done any time after the actual listing of the property. Some preparation is always beneficial. What are some of the things that can be done to set that stage?

Your seller needs to be counseled as to his or her options when the offer arrives. Rare is the market that allows a seller the luxury of rejecting outright any offer tendered by a ready, willing and, most importantly, *able* buyer. It will bear repeating that the ultimate worth of a home is determined by both buyer and seller and very rarely by seller alone.

While on the subject of the offer, this is as good a time as any to forewarn the seller that the price offered by a prospective buyer may not look good at first glance. In soft markets this may be the case even when the home is well priced. The impact will be even more dramatic when the home is overpriced or the seller unrealistic. In either case the seller must be helped over the emotional hurdles of disappointment and possible anger in order to see beyond the price to other terms and to see the offer as a starting point, not a sticking point.

This may be the most critical bit of preconditioning that you can do before actually presenting an offer. The degree to which you are able to persuade and prepare the seller to exercise objectivity over subjectivity, especially regarding offering price, will have a direct bearing on the success of the actual negotiations. Sharing with sellers ahead of time other terms of the sales contract—for example, type of financing, closing date, amount of deposit, inclusions and exclusions—and giving them time to mull over their importance helps to put these issues in proper perspective when the real offer arrives.

The agreement of sale is lengthy and peppered with legal jargon. Introduce the terms along the way to help sellers become familiar with them. Giving sellers the chance to see and read a copy of the sales contract enables them to focus on other details pertinent to the offer when the time comes. Having the opportunity to become familiar with the content of the sales contract and raise questions helps the seller to feel in control. Consider extracting salient points and creating supporting fact sheets, perhaps one to be given with the agreement initially, one to accompany the agreement when the offer is presented and one to be given when the terms are finalized. They serve to highlight what is most important about the form at a particular point in time and describe what it means to the seller. If you've done something similar for the listing agreement, the seller will be looking for your real world translations.

If the home is in the price range of the first-time homebuyer, a brief explanation of seller participation is necessary. This may have been discussed in the course of pricing and possible financing options or in the review of estimated closing costs. If you have not already done so, explain these matters before the offer comes in. Otherwise the issue of seller participation can become an unnecessary stumbling block with sellers who don't understand the importance of their role in this regard.

Time is of the essence where contracts are concerned. Either through explanation or a handout, it's wise to alert sellers to the importance of prompt action. When the offer arrives, they then understand why you may request to present it immediately and the importance of obtaining a response as soon as possible. This is even more important when there are other team members who need to be involved in the discussion or approve the decision. The significance of other time lines called for in the agreement also should be emphasized. Introducing these subjects as well as other local customs and conventions can make a world of difference when the time comes to present the offer.

If you have prepared the seller and family member(s) or other members of the support team for what to expect in an offer, then the actual presentation may be somewhat anticlimactic. And that's okay, even good, because surprising the seller is not your objective. Remember, being prepared means knowing what to expect.

The Nitty Gritty of Negotiating

At this point in the relationship you may find that the senior seller is relying heavily on your advice, especially in the realm of negotiation. While you may be called upon to recommend a course of action or a negotiating strategy, refrain from making the seller's decisions. It can be tempting to direct a seller when he or she cannot seem to reach a decision or when you are directly asked to do so. The degree of dependence on you and your expertise can be great and in spite of best intentions you must be especially cautious with older sellers.

Slices of Life

Also important in the course of negotiating the offer is to recognize the seller's priorities and acknowledge that they may not be the same as yours or even those of the average seller. Consider, for example, the Grabowskis. Although they struggled to come to grips with their need to give up their home due to Mr. Grabowski's increased frailness and inability to drive any longer (his wife had never been a driver), they were interested in and able to handle the arrangements of the move on their own. There may have been a little grumbling along the way about the complexity of the whole process and the details to be attended to, but all things considered it was a smooth and minimally stressful move.

The only glitch came during the negotiation of the offer on their home. The first-time homebuyers had made an offer that after a short discussion the sellers agreed to accept. Although it was less than full price, it was deemed acceptable because of the recognized need for some updating of the property. The home inspection, however, raised concern on the buyers' part about the remaining functional life of the roof. Although represented as older and described by the home inspector as sound at the time of the inspection, the buyers pressed for a new roof. In order to appease the buyers and preserve the contract, the Grabowskis offered a dollar contribution equal to about half the cost of the estimated roof replacement. Still, the buyers, guided by parents in another state, demanded a new roof.

The sellers' agent firmly believed that the original sales price was fair to both seller and buyer, but that a new roof paid for by the sellers would net them less than they could reasonably expect to receive from another offer. The Grabowskis, while upset about the turn of events, still recognized the need to get on with their move as a higher priority. With reluctance—Mrs. Grabowski was more reluctant than her husband—they agreed to incur the additional expense if necessary.

Following the broad definition of "best interests," the sellers' agent would naturally try to protect and enhance the clients bottom line. But it was evident that money was not the most important issue to these people at this time. This type of dilemma is not uncommon. If there had been a family member available to be a part of this discussion, both agent and sellers might have felt more secure in the positions taken.

Interestingly, the Grabowskis did ultimately agree to take a small gamble on the strength of the buyers' commitment to their home. They stood by their offer to pay for half the cost of the roof and the buyers accepted their offer.

Another factor that frequently carries more weight with senior sellers than others is how they feel about the prospective buyers. As Danielle Kennedy says, "Many a house has been sold because the sellers liked the buyers better than the price. People often have a lot of themselves built into the house they can't live in any more, and they want it to go to someone they feel good about." We must be ready to respect the wishes of the sellers when they seek buyers who, they believe, will be good stewards of their home.

Be especially sensitive during the period of negotiations to other priorities of your seller. Be aware, too, that this discussion and its conclusions brings with it the finality of the decision to move. It may be a painful acknowledgment for the seller.

When the Offer Is Slow To Arrive

If the much anticipated offer is not forthcoming in a timely fashion, then, as with any seller, you must be able to produce a record of showing and marketing activity when you set those periodic face-to-face meetings. Thirty-day reports keep the seller posted as well as reinforce feedback and previous recommendations. Regardless of the level of showing activity, be prepared to offer a revised marketing strategy for each 30-day time frame. Don't be tempted to skimp in this regard if the owner has vacated the home. Local or long distance, they need your accessibility and accountability. If a meeting in person isn't possible, it becomes even more important to have current market information in reports that are easy to understand.

Finally, even if price is not the issue and you cannot substantiate the cause for the lack of an offer, you are obligated to balance optimism with an acknowledgment of the hard realities of the marketplace. Both are called for in the course of any listing period. Hard truths cannot be denied and, with so much often riding on these sales, the sellers need to understand clearly what the market is telling them. They may need to reconsider their options and plans if the market will not bear their price.

Between the Contract and the Closing

Sooner or later an offer is received and accepted. While sellers can now focus more fully on their upcoming move, the agent is responsible for coordinating and overseeing many behind-the-scenes details. Once again this is a logical point at which to provide the seller with an overview or checklist outlining what will be going on between the acceptance of offer and final closing. For instance, if inspections are to be completed and an appraisal has been ordered, the seller needs to know that and you may need to be on hand when inspectors or appraisers come to the house. The seller needs to clearly understand what is expected of him or her, what the task will involve and when it must be accomplished.

Despite your best efforts to plan for events leading up to the closing, most transactions bring something unexpected. The better prepared you are for the unexpected, the better able you will be to minimize its effect on sellers who may be consumed with the physical aspects of the move. Perhaps with the senior seller it is best to just expect the unexpected and allow for the necessary accommodations that must be made.

Slices of Life

Sometimes there just isn't anyone else to do what has to be done but you. One of our sellers, Mrs. Rodgers, a careful planner, arranged for her move to a retirement community and hired a service to sell or dispose of the remaining contents of her home. On the day before closing she was dropped off at the house in order to vacuum and gather together some miscellaneous cleaning items. When we stopped to check on her we found her picking away at a small mountain of trash collected in the corner of the basement. There had been a miscommunication regarding its disposal and she was valiantly attempting to move it outside. With no phone, no car and no help, she was upset and overwhelmed by the task. In short order with several extra pairs of hands the trash was bagged and on the curb to await pickup. There was nothing outstanding about being there or doing what had to be done, but sparing the seller the stress at that moment was very important. It was the essence of "being there" for that seller in that transaction and "being there" is a critical component for sellers like her.

Throughout the term of any listing you assume responsibility for its management. Some are more management-intensive than others. By anticipating events and finding successful ways to help the seller prepare for them you can increase your effectiveness without investing your time in repetitive words and actions. By continually putting yourself in the seller's shoes you can work efficiently and, therefore, effectively.

Chapter 7

Teaming Up for Success

A real estate transaction today is so complex that it is impossible for any one participant, including the REALTOR®, to completely understand and handle all facets of the process. For this reason real estate practitioners must rely on other professionals to handle various components of the sale. Think about how many different people touch the transaction from the time a contract is consummated to the time of closing. Each plays his or her part to take the transaction to closing and each can help or hurt you depending upon individual competence and commitment. Your skill and ability to manage this sometimes unruly group may well determine the degree of your satisfaction and success in our business.

Layered on top of the industry's complexities are the life circumstances of the aging American. Considerations such as health, family, money and attitudes are an integral part of the senior's profile. So complexities of circumstances frequently require surrounding these clients with a circle of support in the form of a team when the time comes to sell a home. This support group can make valuable contributions to those facing a potentially hard move. Their value to the REALTOR® can be significant as well; their roles are not unlike those assumed by the teams we already know and use.

The support team might include a member of the client's family, trusted friends and professionals relied upon in previously established business relationships such as accountants and/or financial planners, estate planners or attorneys. Additionally, those newly involved with the client for reasons specifically related to the upcoming move can include a representative from the new residence or community, moving service coordinators or other providers of ancillary services now available to the older population. We'll take a closer look at the makeup of the team and the contributions that each member can make in this chapter.

Why a Team Approach?

The team can benefit all involved in the transaction. How? When assembled correctly this group works in concert to ensure that the right decision for the client is set; ramifications related to finances, taxes and estate planning have been considered; and ongoing support is in place. Each team member has stated responsibilities and brings the specific and complementary knowledge and perspectives necessary to serve the best interests of the client.

Best interests as defined here go well beyond the sale of the home for the highest price, in the shortest period of time with the fewest problems. They include all the ripple effects of the decision to sell a long-established family home. Emotional trauma may be the most readily apparent effect of the decision. Equally important, however, may be the forthcoming lifestyle changes as well as the impact on finances. The REALTOR® is ill-equipped to address most of these issues. There are those who can effectively contribute to this client-agent relationship.

Whether buyers or sellers, senior Americans will need reassurance that the advice you are giving them is sound. They often need help to understand the complexities of the selling and/or buying process. They may need for someone else to accept and assume responsibility for carrying out actions related to the move. They certainly need to understand (or have someone they can trust and depend on understand) the effect of the move on future finances and their estate. And finally, if the move is being made under duress or unhappy circumstances, they may need a lot of emotional support throughout the process and beyond.

Input from team specialists helps to identify and clarify the best courses of action given the special circumstances. Their involvement should offer reassurance to the client. The level of trust between the client and team members, especially those with whom the individual has an established relationship, is usually an asset.

In supporting the client the team also supports the REALTOR®. Their prior relationship with your new client makes them a good source of information for you. They should reinforce your advice and may help carry out activities related to the sale—duties that might otherwise fall to you. The time you stand to gain can be better spent in areas of your greatest expertise, that is, marketing of the property and consummation of a sale.

The resources and professional advice to be found among team members can minimize the need for judgment calls on your part. Of course, the arm's length gained by the members' involvement can be shortened dramatically if you are the one responsible for recommending someone whose advice is later called into question! The following also are other potential liabilities in the use of a team concept:

- Well-intentioned people can become counterproductive team members.
- Both professionals and family members may be out of touch or uninformed.
- They may arrive on the scene too late to fully appreciate the present circumstances.
- You may find yourself in the midst of too many chiefs and too few Indians.
- There is a greater possibility of the need for consensus before taking any action . . . cumbersome and sometimes downright frustrating.
- A weak link may jeopardize the viability and effectiveness of the team.
- If the REALTOR® is the weak link he or she may be revealed as such.
- The participation of a number of people may necessitate some duplication of explanations and communications.

In the final analysis you must assume responsibility for the effective functioning of the team. If this team is to operate as an asset to the seller and to you, you must be the captain. You will need to clarify roles, determine the degree of member involvement and delegate responsibilities. Some of your best negotiating skills may be called into play here.

Selecting the Team

The makeup of the team is as important as its function. The right mix of people gathered together to achieve a common goal assures success in almost any endeavor. Just what does it take to be considered as a candidate for the team? Let's take a closer look at the profiles of possible members *and* the red flags that indicate the need for a particular one.

The Family Member

By far the most available and broadly helpful addition to your team is a family member. In some cases the person serving in this capacity is a trusted friend rather than a relative; the two are very similar for this discussion. It is by design that we begin with the person in this role. This is the one who is potentially your greatest ongoing resource. A relative or trusted friend is a vital addition to the team for a variety reasons.

There is no expectation of real estate expertise on the part of the family member: he or she should bring the client's best interests to the table. Usually a high level of trust exists between the family member and your client and, as we pointed out in Chapter 3, this is the key to the relationship. When you gain the confidence of the family member, you have gained the client's confidence as well.

The ways in which a family member can contribute toward the achievement of the moving goal are many and varied. Certainly, he or she is involved to lend emotional support and may serve as a sounding board and confidant. This person may be called upon to translate or interpret information and decide how it is to be acted upon. Sometimes the family member serves as a buffer, protecting the primary client from information or activity overload by becoming the eyes or ears of the seller, in essence an extension of the individual.

You should be able to count on the family member for insight into the client's words and actions for he or she knows the personality and perspective of the individual well. He or she may also be able to predict the impact of your actions on the client and help to advise you with that in mind.

Indications that a family member should be part of the team:

- The seller's circumstances indicate the necessity to move, but seller's actions and/or words are indecisive.
- The seller seems generally uncooperative and/or argumentative.
- The seller does not seem to fully grasp your explanations.
- Your assessment of the situation indicates the seller may not be able to handle all aspects of the move.

Criteria for choosing a family member or trusted friend:

- Willingness to help
- Level-headed and cooperative temperament

The Attorney

Beyond a family member, the attorney is probably the person with whom you will have the most contact on behalf of the selling or purchasing senior. Reliance on an attorney is likely to be greater if there are no family members close at hand. Attorneys play an important role for two reasons. First, people in the over-55 generation have historically relied upon an attorney to interpret and give blessings to legal documents. While the listing and sales contracts have always been legal documents, in the past they never looked quite as threatening as they do now. The very length of the forms is intimidating due to the depth and breath of subjects likely to be incorporated.

Second, if these sellers are accustomed to running big decisions by their attorney, a pre-existing relationship with him or her will predispose them to involve this resource at this time. It will seem only natural to touch base with the lawyer through the course of the transaction. The contact may be limited to a review of the sales contract or it may be that the attorney actually becomes your contact for any decision of significance. This is true especially if the client is incapacitated in some way or is simply in the habit of asking the attorney for assurance.

An attorney often will be serving as an adviser to the older household, especially if grown children are no longer living in the area. In the children's absence, certain clients call their attorney frequently to check all of the information that has been given to them by other members of the team. In most cases, due to unfamiliarity with the process, they are seeking reassurance. Once again, we are reminded just how overwhelming the sale or purchase of a home is to someone who is not in the real estate profession.

If people are new to an area (moving to be near children, for example) the degree and nature of their use of an attorney varies. In addition to the complexities of a purchase, there may be a more general unfamiliarity with local real estate practices. In some situations clients tend to rely heavily on their children who already live in the area and, in fact, have the children actually make contact with the attorney concerning the many facets of the transaction. Others want to be in frequent and direct contact with the attorney because they have all sorts of detailed questions on the transaction, looking to them for confirmation and clarification of general information as much as legal aspects of the transaction. Such clients are very appreciative of the services received and rely on the attorney to make certain that everything goes smoothly.

Older clients are more likely to rely on the attorney to intercede with other members of the team, even viewing the lawyer as the "captain." This should not present a problem to the agent or to the effective functioning of team. If this professional is appropriately versed in current real estate practice and is willing to be involved as a cooperative participant, he or she will surely be an asset. We need to remember that the client's relationship with the attorney and individual circumstances will determine the nature of this participant's involvement. Frequently, however, the lawyer serves to comfort and assure as much as dispense legal advice.

Indications that an attorney should be part of the team:

- The client does not understand the paperwork or the process, and no family member is readily available to explain and reassure the seller.
- The REALTOR® feels uncomfortable about legal aspects of the seller's circumstances—for example, a question of competency or decisions being made under possible duress.

- The client is accustomed to relying on an attorney for review of legal documents.

Criteria for choosing an attorney:

- Knowledge of current real estate practice and a "deal maker"
- A working relationship with the REALTOR® (Always nice, not always possible!)
- Willingness to work in concert with the team toward the common goal
- Additionally, consider word-of-mouth references and check Martindale-Hubbell legal reference resources and *The Best Lawyers in America.* These books rate lawyers by polling, confidentially, other lawyers.

The Accountant

This potential team member is often the most important one outside the immediate family. The accountant brings the formal dollars and cents perspective to the table. And it is likely that most of those ready to downsize (or make an even trade in terms of money spent for new but smaller living accommodations) have already weighed the decision in light of its financial impact. The accountant will therefore already be in place and your involvement with him or her may be limited to reaffirming that the move has the blessing of this adviser.

How do these financial advisers view the older segment of their business? They confirm that those growing older and moving out of the job market are looking forward to a comfortable retirement. They are at a stage in life where they do not want any debt. There are concerns about having resources to provide for a comfortable life for as long as they may live. And there are concerns about a prolonged illness or nursing home stay. If they have not already done so, they set up or review wills, living trusts and durable powers of attorney. Many set up living wills. Seniors want to get their affairs in order so as to provide for the survivors if married or so as not to be a burden for others if single or widowed.

From the accountant's perspective, the financial and tax decisions facing this group are also more difficult and more varied than those that they had to make earlier in life. Among them are the need for everyone to be in the know about his or her finances, the need for this group especially to carefully consider investment choices, the need to understand and manage retirement dollars and, finally, the need to budget.

Sometimes a surviving spouse has had little experience in handling financial affairs or making major decisions. If that is the case, it is not surprising that such a person would expect to rely on the advice of an accountant, both in reaching a decision to sell a home and in planning for the use of the proceeds of the sale.

Many seniors are so risk-averse that they only look to invest in fixed-income, fully guaranteed investments. They avoid investment risk at the price of inflation risk and the loss of purchasing power. Average life expectancies have increased into the 80s for Americans. If an individual retires at age 65, the joint life expectancy between the retiree and spouse is close to 25 years. For these reasons, it may be difficult but necessary for them to consider holding a purchase money mortgage or using a reverse mortgage or reverse annuity to enable them to stay on in their home. Reverse mortgages and annuities use the principal residence as collateral for the loan. We look at reverse mortgages in more depth in Chapter 10.

And from a tax standpoint, there are decisions to be made. For example: "Should I sell my house to take advantage of the 55 or over one-time exclusion of $125,000 gain from taxation or should I stay in my home? Should I think about retiring to a state that has lower taxes or does not tax pensions?" Any one decision may impact others, sometimes significantly.

The greatest dilemma facing the senior population is that life expectancies are increasing and inflation will always be with us. The earlier that an individual can think about and plan for retirement by saving, the better and more comfortable the retirement years will be. Saving, early and often, will make life easier at retirement.

Closely tied to the longer life expectancies are problems in the future with health care. Many companies do not provide medical benefits to retirees. This added expense must be considered by many retirees and a cash outflow will have to be made. Budgeting, always a good practice, becomes imperative when incomes become fixed and expenses continue to rise. They provide peace of mind.

This, then, is a composite of the client as seen through the eyes of the accountant. We are given a glimpse of the things that these sellers and buyers have thought about and weighed, sometimes over long periods of time. Finally, they reach the conclusion that brings us into the picture. If proper planning did not occur, then we arrive to find a seller at quite another crossroads. It will be most interesting to see what the turn of the century and beyond brings as more and more of us age with less and less by way of social security and pension funds.

Indications that an accountant should be part of the team:

- The client is unsure how the proceeds of the sale will be used.
- The client does not understand the tax implications of the sale.
- You and or the client have uncertainties about this being the time to sell for reasons of finances.

Criteria for choosing an accountant:

- Knowledge of real estate taxation
- Appropriate credentials, such as the CPA designation. Only CPAs can do the things needed.

The Estate Planner

Under the title of estate planner you may actually find a number of disciplines represented. Certified Life Underwriters (CLUs, or insurance agents), attorneys, bank trust officers and accountants all may qualify as estate planners. Regardless of their specific background, these counselors play a vital role in the planning necessitated by those whose assets exceed $600,000, the federal limit on nontaxable assets per taxpayer. Estate planners can provide assistance to taxpayers of more modest worth too, by providing pertinent information on how to best "gift" monies or properties over to a child or other heirs. They can advise about the tax codes of specific states as well.

Exactly what do estate planners do and why are they considered a part of the team? The objective of an estate planner is to assess a client's worth and recommend restructuring of ownerships and assets to reduce the taxes due on the estate. These recommendations must be made in light of the future financial needs of the client. Examples of assets include stocks, bonds, savings, life insurance, pension plans, personal property and, perhaps most importantly from our perspective, real estate. Not surprisingly, the real estate component may play a major role in any discussion with a financial planner.

As part of the financial profile review process, the planner will determine whether the estate is accumulating or contracting, how assets are currently held, including titles to property, and what the wishes, interests and concerns of the client may be. Another part of the process consists of valuing the assets in the estate and formulating a plan for the smooth transfer of those assets to heirs. Minimizing tax impact is part of any smooth transfer.

For example: If a married couple's combined estate showed a worth of $1,200,000, and most of the assets were held jointly, the taxes due on the death of the second spouse would be $235,000. Given the same circumstances, if the client had the foresight to work with an estate planner who advised splitting of the assets, the federal tax impact would have been ZERO. For some taxpayers the savings recognized far outweigh the fees for such advice.

Wills are commonly written in a manner directly in conflict with the way in which title to real property is held. When the will is eventually executed the tax impact on the estate and surviving spouse or heirs is significant. Isn't that information that you would want to be sure that your clients were aware of in making decisions about properties that you were selling to them or for them?

Other asset management vehicles involving real estate also bear mentioning. For example, the creation of a Qualified Personal Residence Trust permits the owner to retain the right to the use of a property for a specified period of time. Ultimately, however, the property is deeded to an heir or designee. The original owner's estate is reduced and the recipient of the property has a more favorable tax consequence. An interesting aspect of this example is that the real estate under discussion could be a second home, possibly set in an attractive location such as a beach, offering the original owner quality retirement living.

Being aware of estate planning vehicles increases the opportunities for selling homes and, most importantly in this context, allows you to recognize the possible need for an estate planner and make an informed recommendation. You can provide a valuable service by recognizing the potential for savings or gain, alerting clients and customers to it and hence to the resource available in the estate planner. Although the need for this professional assistance is more dictated by wealth than age, the need for planning or the likelihood that such things have already been taken into consideration is greater as homesellers and buyers grow older. It is also more likely that, during our work careers, more people will fall into this higher income bracket due to dual careers, inflation and the increasing size of the "upper class." Another consideration is the possibility that the federal government will lower the maximum exemption from the current figure of $600,000. So if you are to be valuable to the people that you want as clients you'd better know what you're talking about and where to direct them for in-depth assistance.

If the magic number is $600,000 stop to consider how many of your customers and clients that might include. Probably more than you might initially think. If the individual you are dealing with is already working with an estate planner then the extent of his or her involvement at the time of the actual sale or purchase of property may be limited. His or her counsel vis-a-vis the sale should already be in place.

Indications that an estate planner should be part of the team:

- The property's value and the client's profile indicate assets in the range of $600,000 or more.
- Other questions asked of the seller indicate uncertainty about use of the proceeds from the sale of the home.
- The client has multiple real estate holdings.

Criteria for recommending an estate planner:

- The individual is qualified by having appropriate experience and credentials, perhaps as an accredited estate planner.
- In states that permit lawyers to specialize, you have a starting point for making recommendations.
- Additionally, consider word-of-mouth references and check Martindale-Hubbell legal reference resources and *The Best Lawyers in America*.

The Moving Coordinator

Think about the kind of support that someone in this capacity can bring as you consider the observations of a popular, local moving coordinator. An organization that specifically caters to the downsizing senior makes the move manageable in a most comforting and reassuring manner. You need to find these services in your market area.

When asked to describe generally how her clientele view their moves, the coordinator responded, "They are ambivalent. They have all the right reasons for wanting to make a move (usually to a retirement community) . . . that is, independence from house and yard maintenance, security, companionship and the life care which is offered by many communities. However, they are reluctant to leave a home that holds most of their memories and where they have raised their children. They are aware that dramatic downsizing means sorting, eliminating and choosing."

She went on to note that, "Many feel unequal to the physical, mental and emotional demands of moving and have no idea where to begin. Very often, their children are occupied with the demands of their own jobs and families, live at a considerable distance, so they are without the necessary support and assistance. We have had clients who finally arrived at the top of a retirement community waiting list and, rather than face moving, considered taking their names off the list."

Moving and all it involves is a major obstacle, especially for older clients. "Other clients, both old and young," she continued, "make a rational decision to change their lifestyle, begin getting organized and just get on with it."

Clients are encouraged to take their memorabilia, their family antiques, their books, whatever gives them pleasure, but to be realistic about what will fit in their new apartment or home. They are also encouraged to "rent a daughter," one of the company's packers, to assist with sorting and cleaning out the cabinets, the attic or the basement, if they need help getting ready for their move.

Other services offered include a consignment and buy-out option for unneeded furniture and household items. However, if in doubt about items, it is recommended that those moving err in favor of inclusion with the understanding that such things can be gotten rid of later. A room planning service enables clients to have a realistic idea of what will fit and where it will go. This service often generates interest and excitement about the positive side of moving, encouraging anticipation rather than regret. With such a plan in front of them they can tell the movers where to place furniture on moving day.

Services like this one allow the person moving to maintain control, but to have support and assistance at every phase of the moving process. As we know, clients run the gamut in terms of personality types. This service provider concludes, "They differ in age, strength, mental acumen, enthusiasm, resources and talents. Many are excited about their new lifestyle and have the strength to prepare. But even the strong tend to be overwhelmed by the details and arduousness of moving."

Those who view moving as a major obstacle find great relief in knowing that there is a reliable resource to help them every step of the way. We need to remember that these sellers face much more than the paperwork and procedures that we bring them. It is incumbent upon us to be ready with resources like a moving coordinator. Of course, financial wherewithal is a necessary consideration and may limit the degree of help available. Hopefully, your tool kit will contain options for most pocketbooks.

Indications that a moving (relocation) coordinator should be part of the team:

- Your assessment of the situation shows a seller bogged down in belongings.
- The seller has no clear plan of action for the physical move.
- The time line for the move is tight.
- No family members are available to help.
- The client is clearly overwhelmed by the prospect of selling the home and relocating to the point of avoiding *any* decision.

Criteria for choosing a moving coordinator/service:

- Reputation in the community
- Recommendations from your business or personal associates
- Membership or affiliation with organizations such as a Better Business Bureau
- Ability to offer a variety of services
- Costs of services

Managing All the Players

The foregoing discussion lists some of the professionals who might become a part of your senior's circle of support. There could be others. It is unlikely that you will be involved with all of these representatives in a single transaction, but it is possible! Whatever the circumstances call for, you need to be prepared to take control as necessary.

In the final analysis the composition of the team will depend upon the specific combination of circumstances of the client and the availability of the resource people needed. In many instances the REALTOR® will still be the one called upon to fill any gaps. Management of the team may be a little cumbersome at times, but each member plays a significant role in the achievement of the ultimate goal. Keep that in mind. This is no time to become myopic or obsessive about control.

Chapter 8

Emphasizing Old Rules, Explaining New Ones

Among the most difficult challenges facing the REALTOR® is understanding and translating the changes that have occurred regarding agency, fair housing and disclosure. These three issues are the most important in purchasing or selling real estate today. As we progress through the 1990s and beyond, the rules will continue to evolve. To stay on top of these changes, agents must make a concerted effort to be informed about many issues and on the alert for changes and additions to laws, public policies and industry regulations. Full understanding only comes with effort and education.

To translate these issues effectively to the senior client, the REALTOR® has to be informed, caring and equipped to deal with emotions tied to moving. Let's look at several of the most significant issues and see if we can help put them into perspective by offering some common dilemmas and their best solutions.

Fair Housing

Let's start with fair housing. This is a top priority in the real estate and mortgage industries. What is it, why do fair housing laws exist and how does it affect me, my company and my customers and clients?

The notion of fair housing first came into play during the Reconstruction period following the Civil War. The Civil Rights Act of 1866 allowed all citizens of the United States the same right to inherit, purchase, lease, sell, hold and convey real and personal property. This law was an outgrowth of the 14th Amendment. Unfortunately, this law was practically ignored and was not enforced.

The Civil Rights Act of 1964 prohibited discrimination in housing that would require government financing or insurance, including those transacted under the FHA and VA programs.

Following was a more expansive law known as the Civil Rights Act of 1968, which protected people from being discriminated against in any housing, based on their race, color, religion or national origin. The familiar block "house" fair housing symbol that permeates newspaper advertising is a creation of this law. In 1974, discrimination by sex was added to the list.

By 1988, handicapped persons, persons with AIDS and families with children were added, but senior citizens were not, thus blocking housing projects, senior homes and the like from being designated for use exclusively to those over the age of 55.

This is the context of the policy that governs real estate transactions. Understanding this brief chronology of fair housing laws is necessary for the REALTOR® to do business now and in the future. Explaining fair housing to clients and customers by using this chronology may well illustrate that these rules, regulations and laws have been in existence long before any of us were born.

Make sure that your client or customer shares your understanding of fair housing practices and is willing to abide by the law. Emphasize that all people have the right to own real estate in whatever area they choose without fear of harassment from others. If you cannot get this commitment up front, you needn't go any further. Walk away: staying will only open you and your broker up to potential liability!

Many of the people we are dealing with today have lived through times when discrimination was the rule, not the exception. This may have even been a dominant attitude when they last were in the market. If these values have been imprinted on them, it may be very difficult to have them come around to our way of thinking, right or wrong.

Slices of Life

Here is an example of a dilemma that was created by a person who didn't understand and didn't accept the principles of fair housing. Early in 1993, Ms. Zimmerman called REALTORS® to place a value on her home and possibly suggest how to market the property for sale. They met a charming woman in her 70s who kept a meticulous home of which she was very proud. Although updating was needed, the house was conditioned to sell quickly.

Ms. Zimmerman was moving to a retirement community and was eager to sell and get on to her new home. She was a planner of sorts and in fact wanted to make the move while still able.

The home was marketed for several weeks and received an offer to purchase that was very attractive and should have been accepted with little discussion. Ms. Zimmerman turned down the offer. This puzzled everyone but nonetheless was her decision. It wasn't full price and may not have matched all of her expectations. Shortly thereafter, the same buyer submitted another offer that was even closer to the asking price. The new offer was not countered but was flatly rejected, as was the first, giving the agents cause for concern. After further conversation with the seller, it became clear that the contracts were rejected because of the buyer's sexual orientation that wouldn't "fit" in this neighborhood. If fact, Ms. Zimmerman didn't want to be disliked by the neighbors because of selling to an "undesirable buyer."

The REALTORS® emphasized the importance of fair housing and how rejecting an offer due to the sexual preference of the buyer could have legal ramifications. Ms. Zimmerman got angry and ceased all communication with the agents from that point forward. The REALTORS® contacted her attorney and explained the situation. He agreed that there was a potential legal problem unless a solution was found. With his aid, the buyer's contract was accepted and proceeded to settlement.

All is well that ends well. Ms. Zimmerman is safely housed in a beautiful retirement community and the buyers are in their new home enjoying peaceful coexistence.

This illustrates that no matter how the agent tries to explain the benefits of fair housing and the potential remedies that may result from violating fair housing laws, the seller's own beliefs superseded what was right. In this instance no matter what the REALTORS® said, they couldn't change values that had been instilled for many, many years.

Now for the solution. Get the adviser, family member, lawyer or even friend to help you explain the importance of fair housing at the onset of the relationship and you will avoid many problems thereafter.

Agency: Who Represents Whom

The subject of agency has just become a major issue in the last 15 years. To understand it, one must know what the term *agency* means.

Perhaps the best entree to clients/customers is to relate agency to other aspects of their lives. For example, a doctor has an agency relationship with a patient that is commonly known as a doctor-patient relationship. An accountant has an agency relationship as he or she is bound to the client, to act in his or her best interest. The client, in turn, pays a fee for that relationship. Attorneys owe fiduciary duties and establish an agency between themselves and their clients. There is a fee attached for whatever services are provided.

Agency in real estate is no different, yet it is perceived as such by many of the public. Traditionally, REALTORS® worked for sellers exclusively and were paid for their efforts. The problem has always been that the buyers who engaged an agent to help find and buy a home thought that this created an agency relationship with the REALTOR®, that the REALTOR® was actually working for them.

The ensuing bad feelings, followed by lawsuits and the drumbeats of consumer advocates prompted our industry to take a proactive stance in disclosing the true nature of agency. In other words, from the beginning it will be determined who is the client.

The movement to full agency disclosure has solved many problems but created confusion both within our industry and the public at large.

The agency relationship is based on one person representing the interests of another person. Real estate agents are licensed by the state to represent a person for the sale or lease of a property. The responsibility of the real estate agent is defined by the state law relating to agents, the REALTORS® Code of Ethics and general principles of agency law.

The type of relationship formed between the agent and the client is a fiduciary relationship. This relationship is one based on trust, because the agent owes the following duties to the client: loyalty, diligence, confidentiality, obedience, disclosure, accounting and reasonable care.

The courts strictly enforce the agency duties so that the client can rely on the agent putting the client's interest before that of anyone else. The courts also require that the real estate agent be fair and honest in all aspects of the transaction.

Until recently, anyone looking for a home to buy had only one way of working with a real estate agent. This involved having an agent or agents show homes on behalf of the seller of those homes. As a customer, the buyer was not represented by anyone except him- or herself. Negotiations over price and terms were entirely the buyer's responsibility.

Now there is another way: Buyer Agency. This method of representation would enable buyers to have a sales associate act on their behalf in all negotiations. This ensures that the buyer's interests are upheld. The buyer will become the client of that sales associate, who will be bound by written agreement to be his or her advocate in finding and buying a home.

In some cities across the United States, buyer agency is employed in an increasing number of home purchases. This form of representation is not mandatory. Buyers may continue to be shown houses by one or more agents who represent the seller and negotiate on their behalf.

Traditional Agency: All Agents Represent Seller

Throughout the country, real estate agents usually represented only the seller in real estate transactions. That meant that all agents were representing the seller, even if one agent was working with the buyer. This was accomplished through a system called subagency. The real estate company that lists the property is called the listing broker. The real estate company working with the buyer is called the subagent, or cooperating broker, because that company actually works through the listing broker. Although the buyer had access to a real estate agent, the buyer had only limited representation.

The agency duties are owed directly to the seller in all transactions where there is no buyer agent. This is true of every real estate company in the United States.

Figure 8.1   Traditional Agency Relationship

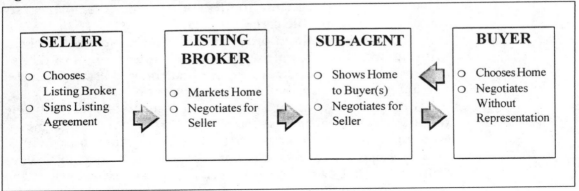

The system has worked well for many years. So long as the buyer is aware that the agent represents the seller, the buyer should not rely on the agent for assistance in determining an offering price that is other than the asking price. Figure 8.1 shows this relationship graphically.

Buyer Agency: Buyer and Seller Are Equally Represented

In real estate transactions, an agency is formed between the broker and the client. The client generally works with one agent who is associated with the broker. The client may be either a buyer or a seller.

Recently buyers have become aware that real estate agents have considerable knowledge that could be of great assistance in deciding what property to buy. In many areas of the country, buyer agency has become as prevalent as the traditional subagency type of business.

When a buyer is represented by an agent, all the fiduciary duties are owed to the buyer and not the seller. The buyer has the freedom to discuss the value of properties, negotiating strategies and personal finances with the agent. The buyer can obtain the opinion of the agent concerning the condition of the property, the effect of improvements, the seller's motivation for selling and other information which a seller's agent should not provide.

A buyer's agent will make a commitment to make every reasonable effort to locate the property described by the buyer. This includes searching for homes that may be available for sale but are

Figure 8.2   Buyer Agency Relationship

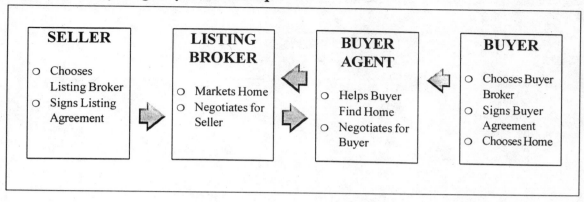

not listed with a real estate company. Although the traditional agent will work hard to find the perfect property for your needs, the traditional agent has some limitations because of the duties owed to the seller. See Figure 8.2.

Dual Agency: Buyer and Seller Are Equally Represented Within the Same Brokerage

A real estate company lists properties for sale, thereby forming an agency relationship with sellers. Throughout the listing period, the seller develops an increasing level of trust in the agent, who is obligated to put the seller's interests first.

The company may also form agency relationships with buyers, who develop an increasing level of trust in the agent, who is obligated to put the buyer's interests first. One example of a buyer agency is an agent working with a close relative, perhaps a mother. It is easy to understand how a mother would expect her son or daughter to give her advice and put her interests first.

A particular broker may be interested in buying a property that is lsited with the same broker, and this situation creates a dual agency. Technically, dual agency arises when one broker has a relationship with two clients who have opposing goals (buyer and seller). Very often the clients are working with different agents who do not have a personal relationship with the other client. When a dual agency is formed, the broker must notify each client.

If a dual agency arises, the clients and agents agree to modify the agency relationship. The agents must not disclose any infor-

Figure 8.3   The Dual Agency Relationship

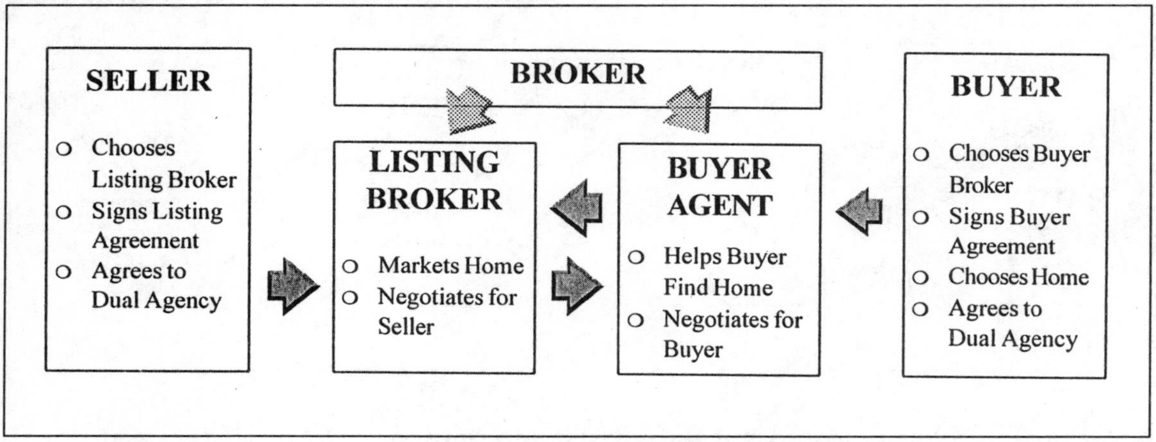

SELLER	LISTING BROKER	BROKER / BUYER AGENT	BUYER
o Chooses Listing Broker o Signs Listing Agreement o Agrees to Dual Agency	o Markets Home o Negotiates for Seller	o Helps Buyer Find Home o Negotiates for Buyer	o Chooses Buyer Broker o Signs Buyer Agreement o Chooses Home o Agrees to Dual Agency

mation that would create a negotiating advantage for either client. The agents must treat the interests of the buyer and seller equally.

Dual agency sometimes happens, and when it does the agency relationship is altered. But everyone's goal remains the same: to buy or sell a property.

Agency will continue to be on the forefront of our industry and agents must be responsible for getting the most current materials on the subject, keeping themselves informed of agency rules and regulations and disseminating this information to the public.

Property Disclosure

Let's switch gears a bit and speak to an issue that has become increasingly important in the 1990s: property disclosure. As recently as ten years ago the words *caveat emptor* rang true throughout the industry as well as the public. This buyer beware mentality put quite a burden on the buyer who didn't know the property as well as the seller. The buyer had no knowledge of problems that may or may not have existed on the property and little idea of what might occur after moving into the property. It also left the buyer with no simple path to remedy any problems.

It is to the benefit of all parties to have full disclosure of the condition of the property for sale. As a matter of fact, it is a matter of law in many states.

Chapter 9

Financing Options for the Over-55 Market

When you service the senior niche, you'll encounter three types of households, each of which requires somewhat different financing approaches and each of which we will deal with in the next two chapters. The first of these types is the younger seniors, whose needs and sophistication will differ little from those of the trade-up buyers a few years younger that you are used to serving. The second group consists of those who are psychologically unprepared to move, either because they cannot face the prospect or because their lives are so bound up with the home that leaving would be tantamount to death. Here, you can use the reverse annuity mortgage (RAM), which we discuss extensively in Chapter 10. Finally, there are those older clients who want to and need to move but cannot see their options clearly.

This chapter focuses on those who will move from their homes and outlines the tools and techniques that are most useful in serving the senior market. It will rehash some ground that's familiar to you—after all, some of your market will differ little from the business you've grown up in. The younger portions of the senior market—those between 55 and 65—are likely to be clients whose patterns and needs differ little from your typical first-time or trade-up buyer. They will be selling a house, usually one they have lived in for a long time, and buying a downsized house suitable to their retirement needs. By and large, they will know the differences between a fixed- and an adjustable-rate mortgage, have heard of Fannie Mae and Freddie Mac and can digest an array of potential mortgage instrument choices.

Some of the material covered in this chapter will be new to this group of sellers, involving either new tools or new ways to use old ones. For many older households—especially those who are not buying again, but rather moving into rental retirement facilities—the full range of options is often unknown and the world of real estate finance is one they have not visited for many years . . . and in that time there have been many changes. As with all other processes in the senior market, taking time to explain carefully the landscape of finance will pay handsomely in making the real estate transaction work. The key here is that financing tools do exist to serve all aspects of the over-55 market.

Attitudes and Attributes

To be successful in serving the over-55 market, particularly in fitting the senior household to the proper financing vehicle, it is helpful to know a little about the manner in which older households approach their housing decisions. From there, the creation of financial strategies is a straightforward move. Let's look at what influences that decision process.

Housing decisions by older Americans are affected by both demographic and financial factors. There are loose connections between these factors and the decision about where to live and how to pay for it, but they remain only generalities. The number of decisions about living arrangements available to seniors—rent or own, independence or dependence, alone or with others—means that demographics and finances are only guidelines to get you on the right road. How you travel on it is much trickier.

Let's begin with the toughest hurdle, the same one we've been dealing with in all aspects of the aging market: attitudes. Most Americans over the age of 55 have been in their current residences more than 20 years. Additionally, most of them have no mortgage on that residence, and the equity in their home constitutes the overwhelming bulk of their wealth.

Only 21 percent of Americans over the age of 65 have any mortgage debt on their house. This figure falls to 8 percent after age 75, and in total 84 percent of senior homeowners carry no mortgage debt. Moreover, only small percentages of older Americans, particularly of those over 65, carry auto or consumer debt. In other words, borrowing is foreign to older Americans and they fund current consumption out of current income.

That pattern of behavior immediately creates a psychological aversion to acquiring more debt, particularly a debt as substantial as a home mortgage. This attitude is strengthened by the emotional attachment to the existing home. Thus, although the house represents a substantial pool of equity that can be tapped to supplement income and fund living expenses, often older households do not see it as such. More importantly, since you will be dealing more with seniors as sellers rather than as buyers, they have little patience for dealing with new financing tools that may be deal makers that sell their homes.

Slices of Life

Take the case of Peg Pierce. Peg and her husband lived for 30 years in a lovely home in a quiet neighborhood. It was nicely suited to their retirement goals and even had ample space to accommodate visiting family and friends. Located near stores and service centers, it was safe and familiar. Best of all, there was no mortgage on the property. Their plan was to travel when Bob retired, but always to return to their home.

But . . . it was simply not to be. Bob died less than a year after he retired. Peg's entire perspective on the home that had provided so many memories and was to be their safe haven for the future changed completely. She recognized the need to revise her housing future. The memories associated with the home were too painful now and its continuing maintenance was overwhelming. So Peg decided to move into an apartment and bank the proceeds from the home sale.

Peg was fortunate in that she had the support of a son and two sisters in her decision making. They agreed with her decision to move and were present during most of the listing process. Peg chose a REALTOR® she had never met, but felt she knew through a weekly radio show; she trusted his opinion on real estate matters. With her support group present, he listed, marketed and sold the property, holding her hand through the entire process.

Peg had many options available to her following the death of her husband. First, she could have remained in the house with the help of a reverse annuity mortgage (the subject of the next chapter). Or she could have sold immediately with no clear plan for the next move. In fact, her personal profile suggests that the latter may well have been her first choice, in the sense that the traumatic loss of a spouse often triggers a quick disposal of the house. That has been, in fact, the conventional wisdom about sudden widowhood. However, it appears that widows are opting to stay in their houses more frequently now than was the case 20 years ago, so perhaps conventional wisdom needs to change.

Peg could have also refinanced the house through more traditional channels, banking and living off the proceeds. Her other choice, the one she actually took, was to sell and move. The financial plans the Pierces had made were sound, even in the case of Bob's death. The outcome served her very well, but only because of the hard work of a real estate professional teamed with a cadre of trusted advisers. While Peg's actions were still highly colored by psychological considerations, now they were guided by good advice.

But older Americans are not a homogeneous group, and their attitudes toward debt and their home differ among subgroups. By far, the most debt averse are the lower-income, single seniors, particularly females. For most of these individuals, any sudden adverse event can create catastrophe because of the thinness of their reserves. So they worry more about ordinary living costs, medical expenses and whether they can afford their home than do other classes of older households.

In particular, the event of widowhood triggers decisions to change the housing arrangement, as was the case with Peg Pierce. For the most part, lower-income and widowed seniors are less likely to move, but if they do, they are unlikely to purchase a new house. Rather, they will give up the homes they own to move into rental accommodations or some sort of congregate facility.

In contrast, younger and more affluent seniors have a more positive attitude toward taking on debt. In fact, among the youngest senior groups (55–65), as might be expected, attitudes toward debt differ little from their middle-aged working counterparts. These households are more likely to adjust to changing housing needs by moving into another owned unit, even if they have built up substantial equity in their current residence.

There are many people like Peg and many others with completely different attitudes and needs. As REALTORS®, we have the opportunity to guide them to their next home and provide the financing means to enjoy it. Take the time to find out the options available, pursue the advantages and disadvantages of each choice and be patient throughout the process. Don't encourage one option over another or try to force the purchase or sale of a property. By taking the time to present the options, you will find satisfied customers and referrals for life.

Strategies and Tools

Let's look at the shape of the current housing finance market. It's dominated by two factors. First, the secondary mortgage market sets the rates and terms that prevail on most types of mortgages. The giants of this market, Fannie Mae and Freddie Mac, are backed by the federal government and now participate in the financing of nearly half of all home mortgages. The second factor is technology. As financial flows can be accounted for automatically via computer, mortgage instruments can increasingly be tailored to individual needs. So, where once the 30-year fixed-rate mortgage was virtually the only instrument available, now there is an almost bewildering variety of options.

These two factors have merged to produce a variety of instruments that are particularly aimed at the senior market. The most comprehensive of these is the reverse annuity mortgage and we discuss this fully in Chapter 10. But there are others, particularly for those households that know they need to move, but are too vigorous to head into a care facility.

They Need To Go, But They Don't Know Where

Often older Americans realize that their house is too much for them to handle, but they remain too vigorous for a nursing home and are unwilling to leave neighbors, friends and family behind to move into a retirement community. Yet the prospect of selling the home and buying another presents the choice of incurring a large mortgage debt late in life or tying up all reserves in a house. The option to move in with family presents itself, but often neither party really wants that to happen, and when it does, friction may result.

A number of options designed for seniors would allow them to avoid these unpleasant alternatives. In the private sector, Fannie Mae offers four separate programs of senior housing opportunities. Two of these are designed to allow seniors to move into separate quarters within the home of relatives, maintaining independence and privacy and still being close to loved ones. The other two would allow the senior to stay in the house, either with the help of a tenant who could maintain the property or with the means to buy maintenance services.

Accessory apartments are completely private dwelling units within a home designed as a single-family residence. *ECHO (Elderly Cottage Housing Opportunity) Housing* is a variation in that the dwelling unit, while on the property of a single-family property, is a separate, self-contained, temporary unit. Fannie Mae enters this market by standing ready to purchase loans made to finance either type of unit, provided that the loans meet certain eligibility criteria, including that the borrower be either the senior or a relative.

Homesharing allows for unrelated individuals to share a home with a senior for the purpose of providing maintenance help. *Sale-leaseback* serves a similar function, in that it gives the senior the capacity to sell the house to a relative and lease it back on a long-term basis. Unlike the first two programs, these options let the senior stay in the house, but provide either physical or financial help in maintaining it.

Again, Fannie Mae will purchase mortgages made for the purpose of setting up either a homesharing or a sale-leaseback deal. It has committed $100 million to these programs, although they have not yet become very widespread. Full information on these programs and the telephone numbers of Fannie Mae's regional offices are provided in Appendix D.

In the public sector, a number of state agencies offering housing programs or services for the aging conduct programs for the benefit of senior housing. Kentucky, for example, provides grants for energy repairs for seniors who own their own homes, and also administers a low-rate mortgage program for borrowers over the age of 62. Appendix A contains the addresses and telephone numbers of the departments of housing and aging in all the states, so that you can get the relevant local information directly.

Serving the Younger Seniors

A great part of the senior market consists of younger seniors who are ready for the last resizing. They are leaving the home in which they raised their childern and relocating to a place of lower maintenance and greater amenities. In general, they are looking for places that fit their chosen lifestyle, but are fairly close to where they now own: most Americans will retire to a place within 50 miles of their current location.

The younger seniors are a very attractive market. Since they are resizing and not selling to move to a retirement or care facility, they offer both sides of the market, sale and listing. These clients are also less skittish about taking on the mortgage debt associated with a new residence. For the most part, they are young enough to be conversant with the mortgage market and understand the ramifications of finance.

But, 30 years seems like an eternity, even to one as young as 55. The standard term of the mortgage market seems beyond any kind of useful planning horizon. Those 30 years will surely encompass a significant decline in income and very possibly the death of one or both partners in the household. Since most retirement incomes offer only a fraction of working pay, the additional encumbrance of a mortgage payment can turn a comfortable retirement into a rather unpleasant experience.

For most home transactions, financing choices are quite simple. A fixed-rate mortgage or a variable-rate mortgage tied to the one-year Treasury bill rate will usually do the job. Of course, there are variations—the usual 30-year term may be adjusted to 15 or 20 years, or the rate may vary with some other index—but for the most part it's a very simple process.

For the older buyer, this is far from the case. Often the variable-rate mortgage is not an option since older Americans either live on fixed incomes or anticipate doing so and would prefer certainty in their mortgage payment. Even for younger families, say those in their 50s, predictability has a real value. In all cases, the time horizon for older households is such that a 30-year term seems unrealistic to both borrower and lender.

The ideal financial strategy to recommend here is twofold. To make the move, the household ought to look at a 15-year, fixed-rate mortgage. This has the dual advantages of allowing for longer-term budget planning and for extinguishing the mortgage early in

retirement. The difference in monthly payments between the 15-
and 30-year terms is not substantial: less than $50 on a $70,000
mortgage, which is probably easily absorbed by the (potential) retiree.

The second part of the strategy kicks in later in retirement,
and that involves planning for a reverse annuity mortgage after the
initial mortgage is repaid. One of the major housing cost burdens
for senior citizens, even if there is no mortgage debt, is the escalating costs of taxes and utilities. The proceeds from a RAM, even
if they are relatively modest, can be calibrated to supplement retirement income in order to offset these costs. Using this two-
pronged approach will establish your expertise and will create a
reputation as a responsible adviser to older households.

The key here is the longer-term planning inherent in the two-
part strategy. Your ability to service the senior household is enhanced if you are able to provide a complete strategy for the financial "endgame" of the household. This, of course, builds on the
team strategy we outlined in Chapter 7.

Wrapping It All Up

The demographic and financial factors determining the
housing adjustments of older households suggest some strategies
for dealing with the financing of housing for this segment that will
push you toward your goal of establishing a niche in the senior
market. The variations within the population of older Americans
suggest that no single approach will work with all.

Of course, no strategy will work without information. We
pointed out earlier the importance of establishing a close relationship and getting to know the characteristics of the client. That
is crucial with older households. The advice you give about selling
and relocating will help only if it meets your client's particular
status and needs.

In the best of all possibilities, financial institutions of all
kinds—banks, pension funds, insurance companies—will develop
"lifetime lending" programs for households of all income levels.
These would allow for the acquisition of housing, education financing, home improvements and retirement income. The marketing advantages are obvious here: the consumer stays with the
same institution and reduces transaction costs through the conversion options offered at every life-cycle stage.

Chapter 10

Building Tomorrow's Business by Helping Them Stay Today

As a REALTOR®, you are likely to have experienced the following situation with both seasoned and younger homeowners. After long hours of work and consultation, you discover that your best counsel is advising the household to stay in the house. In many cases, the owner has borrowed against equity and does not have sufficient wealth to move up or the owner is short on the cash necessary to fund settlement and moving costs. This is less likely for seniors, since statistics show the equity is there. But often they have no good alternative or psychologically simply cannot move.

A Possible Solution: The Reverse Annuity Mortgage

You can keep the family in the home and see to their income needs as well through the use of a rather unusual financing vehicle, the reverse annuity mortgage (RAM), which converts accumulated equity into an income stream that can be used to support the older household in place.

Slices of Life

The call came on a cold winter day. The Rileys had lived in their two-story, four-bedroom colonial for over 25 years and were contemplating a move. Plans were in place, but not in concrete. The chosen location was an apartment in a popular retirement community about two hours distant. A tentative commitment had been made to take it.

From the beginning, the Rileys' ambivalence was obvious. The first comments made—"We don't have to make this move"; "We love our house," "Lived here for 25 years" and "It's a wonderful place to have our kids and grandkids come to play and stay"—all raised red flags. All four children lived locally and the importance of family was apparent. In fact, the Rileys had converted their large family room into a dining room to accommodate everyone during regular gatherings. What had been the dining room was now a den. They noted that it roughly matched in size the "living room" in the new apartment—if they decided to move.

The first visit to the Rileys' home was most telling. They wanted to anticipate their future needs and avoid becoming a burden to their children. They had friends of many years living in the new community, but just as many living in the old neighborhood. They had close ties to a local church and their interests were many and varied. What do you as a REALTOR® do in this case? Strange as it may seem, you might want to talk the client out of selling.

Probably the hardest situation to deal with involves the single individual household that is being pressured by family and friends to move out of a house that he or she can no longer maintain for either physical or financial reasons. The emotional attachment of the home is such that the individual cannot bear to leave, and the care facility alternatives are premature, yet the financial picture seems overwhelming. So you are called in to sell the home.

This is a case where your long-term success may rely on turning down the listing. If the seller is not truly motivated, your job becomes stuck somewhere between difficult and impossible. Rather, it would be better to work with the family to look at a reverse annuity mortgage or a purchase money mortgage (PMM). In this case, you will resolve a family dilemma and gain trust that will result in later business for you. You've turned down a sale, but created a relationship. And with senior Americans, real estate is a relationship business.

FIGURE 10.1   Characteristics of Most Likely RAM Users

Characteristic	Comment
Lower income	High value on additional income from RAM
Wish to stay in homes	RAMs provide the means
Low desire to bequeath	Preservation of equity not a concern
Reasonable equity position	Necessary to create cash flow
Older household	Over 75s reap greatest benefit
Long tenure	Equity grows over time
Single applicant	Life expectancy factor lower, leading to higher payments
Accepting of debt	After all, this *is* a mortgage

The reverse annuity mortgage converts the home equity built up over the years by the homeowner into a stream of payments that can be used for supplementing other income, funding necessary maintenance or at-home health care, or providing family gifts. More important, it helps overcome the greatest barrier between the real estate professional and the older client: the homeowner is allowed to age in place without the stresses of keeping up an aging property. Figure 10.1 shows the characteristics associated with users of the RAM vehicle.

While RAMs are not particularly new, they have not been in much use. The reasons are fairly straightforward. For the lender, the RAM is a pain: clients live too long or the house drops in value. For the borrower, ceding control of the home is a scary occurrence, and may not meet with favor from the heirs who stand to inherit the property. In fact, very few people even know about the existence of RAMs, much less their advantages.

Now, however, government and private programs are beginning to blossom, probably in response to the growing number of seasoned homeowners, together with new mortgage technologies that allow for easier computation of loan terms.

The U.S. Department of Housing and Urban Development (HUD), through the Federal Housing Administration (FHA), has initiated an experiment in which it authorized the insurance of 25,000 Home Equity Conversion Mortgages (HECMs), its version of the RAM. In the private sector, a number of financial institutions, having remedied some earlier flaws in the loan process, have entered the market with the aim of creating a niche. Later in this chapter, we describe both of these programs.

In its nuts and bolts, a reverse annuity mortgage allows a homeowner to transfer equity in the home to a lender in return for a series of periodic payments, either preset or determined by the borrower, who draws on a line of credit. The RAM is attractive in that it is an extremely flexible instrument and can be tailored to the specific needs of the household. For example, a borrower can receive monthly payments from the lender for as long as he or she lives in the home; this is called the *tenure option*.

In this case, mortality tables (easily obtained at any insurance office) are used to figure the time period of the payments. If the borrower is 70 years old and expected to live to age 89 (approximately current life expectancy), the payments are figured on a 19-year basis. This opens up one of the major risks attached to the RAM. If the borrower outlives the mortality tables, he or she receives more than the amount agreed upon and the lender loses. If the borrower dies before expectations, the lender receives a property for less than it had originally expected to pay.

If the *term option* is chosen, the borrower contracts for a certain number of payments. Outliving the contract is a distinct negative in this type of arrangement. In that case, the payments cease, and the property reverts to the lender. The borrower, by now far more aged than at the time the contract was signed, is left with no income stream and no house.

This is a potential negative for the lender as well, as the public image of evicting octogenarians is hardly flattering to a bank. In addition, the threat of a suit from the potential heirs is quite real. Ironically, the older the borrower, the less these risks loom on either side. The income stream to the borrower is larger and the mortality tables more accurate. Nonetheless, as you counsel your senior clients, it is imperative to point out these peculiarities of the RAM.

Finally, the borrower may elect the *line of credit option* and draw cash at times and in amounts he or she chooses. This is extremely useful to the household that has income sufficient for ordinary living expenses but is seeking to insure against the shock of a major medical bill or needs to make major repairs to keep the house in liveable condition. In this sense, the RAM can be thought of as an elderly equivalent of the home equity loan.

The FHA–HECM Experiment

As we mentioned earlier, the federal government, through the Federal Housing Administration is currently insuring the value of RAMs on an experimental basis through the Home Equity Conversion Mortgage program. FHA is authorized to insure 25,000 of the mortgages originated through the end of 1995. Insurance is available to borrowers 62 and older who own residences meeting FHA's minimum property standards and who agree to receive counseling from an independent entity. As of mid-1992, only about 2,500 HECMs had been insured.

The loans may be at fixed or variable-rates. The latter, of course, are more difficult to compute since the RAM has the nature of a fixed payment annuity. HUD handles this problem by using a fixed mortgage interest proxy, called an *expected average mortgage interest rate* to determine the initial balance and the compounding rate.

HECMs are secured by the value of the house; the proceeds to the borrower depend primarily on the value of the house and the interest rate on the loan. The borrower can choose any of the three payment options outlined earlier. If the borrower chooses the *line of credit option*, HUD determines, based on the value of the house, a maximum amount (called the *principal limit factor*) available to the borrower immediately.

But unlike uninsured RAMs, the borrower who chooses the *term option* under the FHA-insured HECM is not required to move out of the house at the term of the loan. Rather, the payments stop, but interest on the outstanding balance accumulates until the house is surrendered. Of course, this opens up the possibility that the amount owed exceeds the value of the property.

The counseling requirement of the FHA program is aimed at providing borrowers a full explanation of the details of RAMs and the alternatives they may choose. In addition, counseling helps borrowers understand the full impact of the loan on their current and future financial status, including their estate. This counseling must be provided by a third party (independent of borrower and lender) approved by HUD.

All insured loans must be secured by principal residences that meet HUD's minimum property standards. Should the property fall short of these, part of the loan proceeds can be used to finance repairs. Repairs necessary to bring the property up to standard costing less than 15 percent of the property value may be deferred until after closing. Cooperative housing is ineligible for RAM financing, and condominiums qualify only if they meet HUD standards.

Like all RAMs, HECMs carry risks to both the borrower and the lender. The program has built in some protections that are aimed at minimizing the impact of these risks. The basic protection to the borrower is the federal insurance. Regardless of the mortgage principal balance or the value of the house, the borrower will never be forced to sell in order to pay off the mortgage, and liability at the point of sale is restricted to the value of the house. Should the lender fail to make the contracted payments, HUD will assume the burden of those payments, even acquiring the mortgage should the lender completely fail.

For these protections, the borrower pays an FHA mortgage premium consisting of two parts, both of which are eligible to be financed under the HECM. The first part is an up-front premium equal to 2 percent of the property value. Second, the borrower pays an annual premium, in monthly installments, equal to ½ percent of the outstanding loan balance.

The FHA insurance is key to increasing the use of RAMs. One of the major risks facing lenders with a RAM is that the property will decline in value. When the property is eventually sold, the proceeds may not be sufficient to repay the mortgage debt. The risk is particularly great since most of the units with a RAM will be old and their owners less able to keep them up. With federal insurance, the lender will be more willing to grant this loan. If you have a customer who could benefit from a RAM, investigate the FHA program.

At present, a number of private institutions are moving vigorously into the RAM market, sensing the growing demand for this product. The demographics suggest that the RAM is at about the same market position as the adjustable-rate mortgage (ARM) in 1980. The widespread acceptance of the variable-rate mortgage now may well mean a similar use of RAMs by the end of the decade.

Conclusion

Since the reverse annuity mortgage is contingent on the lifespan of the borrower and the value of the property, the income stream from the mortgage will vary greatly, and with it the attractiveness of the mortgage. Clearly, the periodic payments to the borrower under a RAM will be greater for higher value houses than for less expensive properties. But they will also be greater the more the property is expected to appreciate. Payments will be greater when interest rates are low than when they are high, since the lender factors in the current rate when calculating the periodic payment.

In addition, because their life expectancy is less, older borrowers will receive higher periodic payments than younger ones. This is, ironically, one area where seniors have the market edge.

The major drawback to the RAM for the borrower is the risk of outliving the payments. The mortgage specifies a termination date at which the house must be sold. The periodic payments are calculated to exhaust the value of the house at that point. The lender then sells the house and, presumably, receives back full value for the loan.

If the borrower is still alive at that time, he or she must find other living arrangements and fund them out of current income. The FHA program precludes this possibility and is therefore more attractive to most older households than are conventional programs.

The fear of being elderly and homeless makes most older Americans reluctant to give up the homes they own and live in and has thus restricted the use of RAMs to tap into wealth. As you deal with likely candidates for a RAM, be aware that the psychological barrier of future destitution is a major hurdle.

Chapter 11

Finding and Capturing the Older Market

In the preceding chapters, we've looked at the general size and motivations of the senior market, the problems facing the REALTOR® who decides to enter this market and a host of tips to help you prosper. What's missing is how to find and enter this market. That's what this chapter is all about.

Identifying the Market

The initial step is discovering where this market is concentrated. In most areas, whole neighborhoods developed during the 1960s retain their original residents. These are usually suburbs conducive to—even designed for—raising kids. They are physically mature and convenient to schools, shopping and jobs. And they are about to turn over. The original residents are nearing retirement or resizing age (the nest is empty and the house doesn't quite fit anymore). In many cases, large numbers of houses in these neighborhoods are likely to turn over in a short period of time.

Now you probably know your market area quite well, and on reflection could identify these areas easily. But real estate professionals, involved with the first-time buyer or trade-up market niches, too often look past these neighborhoods. The houses are older, the rooms inconveniently configured and the decoration too dated to appeal to younger buyers. Yet if you're looking to establish an identity in the over-55 market, these are the very best neighbor-hoods to farm.

Of course, you could broadcast your message throughout your market area, but that would be using a shotgun where a rifle is more appropriate. The result is likely to be frustration when the business payoff from the broadcast is weak. You'd be better off to zero in on these markets by starting with the broadest overview of the population, which is provided by the federal government. The Bureau of the Census breaks down the country into census tracts, areas containing approximately 10,000 people. For each of these tracts, the decennial census data are organized by population and housing characteristics.

You can use the census data to analyze any given area by the age of the residents, their incomes and the year they moved into their current house. Crossing over to the housing side, you can look at the types of houses in a given tract, the degree of owner occu-pancy and the physical condition of the buildings.

Putting this information together will give you a clear picture of where the senior community resides, for how long and in what condition. If you find a census tract where there is a high per-centage of older citizens who have lived in their homes for a long time, with a high percentage of owner occupancy and a solid housing stock, you've found a prime senior target market area. Your efforts to promote yourself and generate listings and sales will be efficiently used here.

The problem is that census data are, well, dated. We get ten-year snapshots of the American public, and we only get them after two years. So, the *1990 Census of Population* first appeared in 1992, and now, halfway through the decade, is not completely on point. An alternative, particularly for those involved in real estate, is the American Housing Survey. This comes out every three years and omits many of the population statistics. It is done at the metro-politan level, and thus is less targeted than is the census data, but is fresher in age.

It is useful, however, only for those doing business in metro-politan areas.

Poring through statistics may not be something that interests you, but the census and American Housing Survey data are available in a variety of accessible formats. In addition to hard copy, the information is available in computer tape, CD-ROM and micro-fiche formats. A number of firms also take the census data and break it down to suit your individual needs. To find out about the full range of Bureau of the Census data products, call the customer service line at 301/763-4794. Ask for the *Census Catalog and Guide,* which is published yearly. To find out about firms that specialize in sorting and organizing census data, pick up a copy of *American Demographics* magazine.

After you've used the government data to target the senior market, the next step is to investigate more specific local conditions. At the state level, housing agencies and agencies on aging will point you toward the local facilities that focus on senior citizens. These include public centers, local tax abatement offices and private groups such as churches. Often, these organizations will have mailing lists available that you can use to reach the potential senior market. In Appendix A, we've listed by state the housing agencies and agencies on aging. These are the main sources for county-level information.

Finally, look to the malls. Large regional malls often allow clubs of seniors to use the common areas for walking as exercise prior to business hours. When we discuss prospecting below, we constantly refer to going to the market, that is, providing activities accessible to the senior market. This often means going where the clients are. Finding them is a key to entry into the senior market.

Prospecting the Market

Having looked at all the local statistics available and found the concentrations of seniors in your market area, your next step is to find out who they are and have them find out about you. Since this is a particular market niche, broadcast advertising will not work: it is costly and the message cannot be sufficiently tailored to be heard. But there are other ways to farm this market, and one in particular has been proven extremely effective.

Hold a Seminar

Probably the best way to meet seniors and help establish yourself as a caring expert in this market is to hold local seminars. For the most part, the market you are looking for is inhabited by people who have an excess of time, discretionary wealth and a keen interest in investing it wisely. So the opportunities abound.

These seminars can set you apart from other agents and position you as the expert in the senior market. Positive responses from one session can ripple out through senior networks to the entire community.

Teaching several of these classes over the past six years has afforded one of the authors, Buddy West, the opportunity to meet and help many seniors who were either class participants or referred by the seminar participants. His classes have focused on a variety of subjects related to the housing and financial situations of older households, including making the "stay or go" decision, over-55 tax treatment of housing, housing alternatives for seniors and preparing for downsizing.

Seminars have proven lucrative and helpful to the participants as well. Seniors all over the country are avid for information on financial planning and housing choices from reliable sources. So often are they the target of scams and swindles that the ability to get advice from a known, reliable source is extremely attractive.

In preparing a successful seminar, a variety of factors need to be considered. First, location and time are extremely important. Most seniors do not like to travel a great distance for information and prefer to be home at an early hour. So plan the seminar in an easily accessible, central location and hold it during the day, preferably late morning. Senior centers, malls and churches are particularly attractive because these facilities are likely to be familiar to your target clientele. Be sure that the seminar location is handicapped accessible and well-lit: security is a key concern for older Americans.

Second, advertise the seminar in local newspapers and other publications likely to be read by seniors. Posters in senior haunts like churches, lodge halls and senior centers, particularly those close to the seminar site, will be very helpful. Department stores are also an option. Advertisements are sometimes paid for by the store and carried in the local newspaper. The association of the seminar with a larger education program carried out under the auspices of a known business adds to the legitimacy and attractiveness of the seminar.

Third, consider the material. It must be meaty enough to be seen as more than an advertisement, yet simple, direct and of obvious use to the audience. The seminar conducted by Buddy West consisted of four classes. Two were geared toward first-time homebuyers (and thus were not aimed at the senior market), while the other two focused on housing questions facing the older household. The audience for these last two sessions was remarkably varied. Most of it consisted of people over 55, but there was a strong representation of people in their 40s who were either assessing options for their parents or planning for their own futures. All members of the audience wanted as much information as possible, but more importantly, wanted to be kept aware of any future developments. The result was a marketing list that was focused and effective.

You can increase interest in your seminar if you can attract a guest speaker, one who is known by the audience as an informed source. You don't need to book national names; local experts will do nicely. An accountant can explain the tax consequences of disposing of property, particularly the regulations surrounding the over-55 capital gains tax exclusion. Attorneys can speak to the importance of a will and its effect on owned real estate. An estate planner can expand on this into the full range of asset disposition strategies. Can you pull such a panel together? Sure you can, but bringing in an expert makes you look more connected to the information community in your area. In fact, if you have formed a team, as we discussed in Chapter 7, its members can be your faculty and promote business for the entire team.

If you do deal with guest speakers, make sure that the presentations are interesting, brief and in lay terms. Handouts are always helpful, and make sure you leave sufficient time for questions and answers. The value of any session is the information participants get that is directly relevant to their specific concerns. By all means, remain in control of the seminar as its leader and act in a support capacity to any invited presenters. It is very helpful if you have an outline for yourself and any guest speaker to ensure that the class flows. As your audience asks questions, encourage them to give input on personal circumstances. This breaks the ice among the participants, and also gives you some insights into particular needs you can serve.

Fourth, consider the seminar cost. We have found that free seminars don't really work. The perception, particularly among older households, is that "if it has no cost, it has no value." Charge a small fee to help defer the cost of the room, materials and advertising. Don't expect to recoup all your costs; this might make the fee prohibitive for seniors and defeat your purpose. If you can prepare a handout that participants can take with them—a planning guide, a list of other information sources, addresses of local agencies and experts—it increases the perception of value and balances the fee. We've found that $5 to $10 for a two-hour seminar is reasonable and doesn't chase away the audience. In the best case, you can fit your sessions into a larger program, where the sponsoring entity—in this case the department store—sets the fees and collects them, taking you completely out of the money picture.

Finally, follow up each and every attendee. At the seminar, hand out an evaluation sheet for participants to fill out and return at the end of the session. The sheet contains a questionnaire about the session, space for any follow-up questions they would like to have addressed and their names, addresses and telephone numbers. If you have a personal newsletter, include a check-off box for those who wish to receive a copy and ask whether they would like a personal consultation about their housing needs and questions. The next day, send a personal letter to thank each participant for attending the seminar and enclose three business cards along with your personal promotional brochure. Ask for the names of others they know who might be interested in attending a future seminar.

In sum, the seminar process breaks down into seven steps:

1. Choose the location.
2. Pick the time.
3. Craft an outline.
4. Invite any guest speakers.
5. Advertise the seminar.
6. Prepare class materials (handouts, evaluations, questionnaires).
7. Follow up (letter, phone call, personal visit).

The seminar is a highly effective method of reaching a broad spectrum of older Americans, particularly younger seniors who are more affluent and more in control of their housing choices. It allows you to develop a highly targeted farming list and positions you as an expert on the needs of seniors and who cares about their problems and concerns.

Host a Health Walk

Another effective approach to the senior community is to sponsor a health walk. This activity can take place outdoors in a recreational area if weather permits or at a local mall with the owner's permission. A twist on this prospecting idea is to go to a mall where seniors walk for exercise and offer a juice break station for the walkers. If you use travel cups imprinted with your own personal advertising, the walkers take you with them. If you can afford plastic travel cups, the shelf life of your impact increases dramatically.

Expand on this idea and sponsor a senior Olympics event in your area. These are established and run by specific groups that can be identified through the local agency on aging. The events range from bowling to baseball and provide an excellent opportunity to get your name known in the senior community and network with the senior audience.

Organize a Lifestyle Tour

Many people over 55 or approaching that age are concerned about future living arrangements and a change in their lifestyle. It seems logical that planning is the easiest way to adjust to the eventuality of moving, but people tend to deny this reality, putting decisions off until they absolutely have to be made. At that point, simply getting information on options, much less choosing among them, is extraordinarily difficult. That difficulty opens an opportunity for you to become known and respected among seniors by exposing the options at a point where planning is still feasible.

This can be done by sponsoring a lifestyle tour around your market area. The idea is to show seniors a variety of housing arrangements offered in the area. These can be varied by price, degree of independence, services provided and location. Often, local retirement communities, senior centers, banks, mortgage companies and developers of senior housing will participate in the tour as a joint venture with you. The essentials of the tour are quite simple:

1. Pick a date.
2. Arrange for transportation (check into senior center or Red Cross vans).
3. Coordinate lunch at one of the stops (this gives that facility a chance to show off its kitchen).
4. Advertise the tour.

Because the purpose of the tour is to provide information, each of the developments and facilities the tour visits should provide literature describing the housing and care options available. But the tour is also designed to promote you, so have your own materials available to the tour attendees. An added bonus here is that your name is being circulated not only among the senior community, but also among bankers and developers who deal with the elderly and the managers of care facilities designed for them. Future business will come from these sources as well.

Sponsor a Community Health Check

A proven winner in senior prospecting is the community health check. It's a great way to develop contacts among older households while it provides a terrific service to this market niche. Offer the participants a free blood pressure, cholesterol and pulse check. Contact a local hospital, health clinic or the Red Cross to supply a registered nurse to perform the actual screening and then choose a highly visible spot to set up a tent for the testing. Better yet, secure a mobile unit to go into neighborhoods with high concentrations of older residents. Advertise the time, date and place, and personally orchestrate the event.

As a follow-up, it's always a great idea to provide all attendees with a token of appreciation to take with them, for example, a health tip card, a sipping cup, a sweat band or some other small related item. It never hurts to use those giveaways as a means of promoting yourself personally. Your picture, telephone number and address are always valuable reminders.

The Bottom Line

Many other ideas can be implemented in farming the senior market, some of which are simple adaptations of your mainstream farming materials. The key is targeting. Before any sales promotion can be used, the location of the market must be fixed. There are not so many senior citizens in any area that a broadcast appeal will be cost effective. This is one area where research and preparation pay off grandly. Look to the census data (or pay someone to do it for you) and pinpoint those neighborhoods that are the most fruitful farming areas. Then be inventive and craft marketing pieces and events that really appeal to this market.

Chapter 12

A Menu of Materials To Ensure Success

We trust that the information presented in these chapters has introduced this market to you in some depth and provided you with insights about the people who populate it. What follows is a handbook of materials that we have designed and adapted from other sources to use with our sellers. Although we use most of the information with all of our sellers, some of it was developed specifically for our senior clients. Their questions and the input they have provided us over numerous transactions formed the foundation for what follows.

With necessary adaptions for your business practice and location, the information set forth in this chapter will give you some useful resources without the need for quite as much research!

Why To Use Handouts, Charts, Graphs and the Like . . .

These support materials reinforce information that you want the seller to understand and remember. If you sequence the presentation of pertinent material in such a manner that it arrives just ahead of the event, it will introduce the subject, save you explanation time, sometimes "pre-sell" the recipient and other times educate. For example, to secure your position as the agent of choice, provide the prospective seller with a resume plus an overview of sales records and testimonials, especially those from similar sellers.

We also educate and pre-sell the seller on matters such as the importance of proper pricing by introducing him or her to the market, overviewing it, showing the average time on the market (in general and specifically in the price range and geographical area of the subject property) and describing what the available inventory looks like. We also explain in print (in more than one format) what it takes to get a house sold and why houses don't sell.

The pricing presentation is bound as a report and the market analysis is reinforced with information that is easy to read and understand. We work to make the market meaningful and resist the temptation to bury the seller in meaningless numbers. The goal is to use straightforward composites of information that lead to logical conclusions.

As the listing is signed and thereafter, the goal is helping the seller to be prepared for what is to come. We break the process into time sequences and deliver information about what's going on and likely to happen during a given time frame.

Here's What Follows

Prelisting Packet

- Introduction—Overview of packet contents
- Our Commitment—Business philosophy and introduction to the market and pricing
- Choosing Your REALTOR®—Things to look for in a good agent
- Reference List—Short list of former clients
- Testimonials—Comments from former clients
- Calendar of Events—Explanation of pricing research and presentation of recommendations
- Exclusive Services—Special services provided
- Importance of Pricing—Visual reinforcement of this critical point
- What Determines Value—Clarification of common misconceptions
- Pricing/Showings/Offer/Sale—Visual reinforcement of these relationships

The Pricing Presentation

- Cover Page—Customized for the seller
- Seller Sets the Price—Reinforcement of buyer's role in the selling process
- Houses Sell Quickly—Price/market time relationship
- Activity Bar Chart—Reinforcement of pricing/showing activity relationship
- Average Difference Between—Relationship between proper price/selling, price/time on market
- Comparative Market Analysis
- Pricing To Sell—Relationship between pricing and available prospective buyers
- Sellers Estimated Closing Costs

Listing Materials

- Homeowner's Homework—Things for the seller to do
- Record of Showings—Log for seller to keep
- Marketing Plan—Schedule of marketing activities
- What To Expect—Explanations of activities and procedures
- Showing Activity Report—Computerized report for the seller
- Putting Your Home to the Test—Explanations of inspections and related issues
- Glitches—Issues that come up close to the closing date
- Seller's Check List—Details for the seller to handle prior to closing
- Moving List—Items to take care of before and after a move

Prepared for Tom & Carol Hawley

INTRODUCTION

This information is provided to you in advance to help
you compare us with other agents. It is designed to:

* Introduce us to you and establish our
  credentials.

* Suggest to you objective criteria for
  choosing a realtor.

* Profile Patterson Schwartz, the company,
  for you.

* Explain to you how we arrive at a listing
  price for a home and how we prepare a
  home for marketing.

* Describe to you some of the exclusive
  services that we provide for our sellers.

* Show you statistically what the real estate
  market is like today in New Castle County.

* Give you a brief introduction to the
  importance of a proper pricing strategy
  to achieve the results you want.

Prepared by Betsy & Buddy West, CRS's, GRI's
Patterson Schwartz & Assoc., Inc.

Prepared for Tom & Carol Hawley

OUR COMMITMENT TO YOU

When we meet to discuss the sale of your home you'll have to decide in a matter of several hours or so, whether to trust the sale of the single most important asset you own to us. In the attached information and in our pricing presentation, we will provide you with enough information about the market, our qualifications and our marketing program for you to make an informed decision about who will best represent you in this important business transaction.

Our objective is to provide you with accurate and timely information about the real estate market in our area so that you can make intelligent decisions regarding the sale of your property. We will tell you what you must hear and not what we think you may want to hear about the market and the value of your property as it relates to the market. We will substantiate all of our recommendations and conclusions with factual data that we have extracted from the Multiple Listing System.

It may be that you want to get an opinion from another agent and that's fine. However, you should know that all agents have access to the same information. Therefore, the determination of value should be very nearly the same. Remember, no agent can affect market conditions and to suggest that you can sell your property for other than what the market indicates it is worth is a disservice to you and only prolongs the sales process and, according to the National Association of REALTORS® statistics, results in a lower net proceeds amount.

The best way to avoid this situation is to select your REALTOR® based on experience, reputation and results. If you truly want to sell your home, you must be willing to sell it for what the market will bear. If you are not, that's perfectly okay and perhaps we can help you in the future when and if the market changes in your favor, but if you want to sell now, no one will provide you with more candid feedback and factual data than we will. In addition, we will thoroughly explain our marketing program to you and show you how it has worked well for others. We have also included the names of several recent clients with whom we have worked so that you can discuss our credentials with someone who has had first hand knowledge of the way we work.

We are professionals in every sense of the word and our commitment to you is that we will provide you with the best possible service available so that your goals are met in the most reasonable time frame possible. We want you to be satisfied with the final results and pleasantly surprised by our responsiveness and attention to detail.

Prepared by Betsy & Buddy West, CRS's, GRI's
Patterson Schwartz & Assoc., Inc.

Prepared for Tom & Carol Hawley

CHOOSING YOUR REALTOR

IS THE SALES AGENT . . .

... experienced, with over 25 years in the Real Estate industry?
... a full time REALTOR®?
... knowledgeable about market trends in your community?
... a lifetime member of the New Castle County Million Dollar Club?
... a licensed broker?
... a member of the #1 producing real estate office in the state?
... recognized in the top 3% of agents nationwide?
... someone with whom you feel comfortable?
... someone that you can trust and who will uphold your best interests?
... someone who will be honest with you always?
... someone who is genuinely enthusiastic about marketing your home?

HAS THE SALES AGENT . . .

... completed a comprehensive market analysis of your property?
... provided a complete pricing presentation?
... provided printed copies of all data and documentation?
... clearly outlined for you the selling process?
... provided references?
... provided a detailed list of recommendations for staging your home?
... promised a written, customized marketing plan?
... committed to predetermined verbal and written communication?

DOES THE COMPANY THAT SUPPORTS THE AGENT . . .

... consistently boast the largest market share in New Castle County?
... represent more buyers and sellers than any other New Castle County firm?
... generate numerous buyers on reputation alone?
... stay open for business 7 days a week to handle inquiries?
... offer continuous advertising through its Real Estate Hotline?
... have its roots in Delaware? Has it been Delaware owned, Delaware managed
and committed to the community it serves since 1961?

Prepared by Betsy & Buddy West, CRS's, GRI's
Patterson Schwartz & Assoc., Inc.

Prepared for Tom & Carol Hawley

We can provide you with a list of some of the people we've served ...

... You're welcome to call them.

Name	Address	Phone
Carla & Dennis Zajac	8 Basswood Drive	992-3270
Lynne & Don Brown	401 Hawthorne Drive	762-4344
Nancy & Joe Nemecz	302 Jackson Blvd.	428-1532
Penni & Gary Gioffre	30 Paschall Road	762-1907
Mary & Joe Nester	429 Haystack Drive	325-7207
Nancy & Jeff Johnston	550 Red Fox Circle	800 282-8590

Prepared by Betsy & Buddy West, CRS's, GRI's
Patterson Schwartz & Assoc., Inc.

Prepared for Tom & Carol Hawley

TESTIMONIALS

"Buddy and Betsy West do a remarkable job in marketing a home and continue to amaze us with their courteous and professional services. Buddy and Betsy certainly illustrated that they were both willing to go the extra mile in providing complete service to their clients."

Norman and Marcella Loebensberg
Wilmington, Delaware

"Betsy and Buddy West worked harder than any agent we've used in the past (and we have moved a lot so we have good comparisons)"

Bill and Rita Kuenstler
Fort Collins, Colorado

Buddy and Betsy West were a pleasure to work with. They were more than helpful and pleasant."

Mr. and Mrs. Robert Beeman
Wilmington, Delaware

"Our listing agents, Betsy and Buddy West, have been consistently helpful, professional and energetic in their efforts to market our home. From the initial market analysis to the final settlement, Betsy offered advice and support that helped us to expedite our sale."

Ashby and Nancy Richards
Brunswick, Maine

"Every facet of the resale was handled professionally. All advice and counsel was excellent. Buddy and Betsy West are the absolute best."

Mr. and Mrs. Joseph McDivit
Galena, Maryland

Prepared by Betsy & Buddy West, CRS's, GRI's
Patterson Schwartz & Assoc., Inc.

Prepared for Tom & Carol Hawley

Buddy West, CRS, GRI

Memberships, Recognitions, Activities
1995	Director, Delaware Assoc. of REALTORS®
1991 to 1995	Director New Castle County Board of REALTORS®
1990 to present	REALTOR® of the Year Committee

Delaware Association of REALTORS®
1991 to 1995	Convention Committee (Chairman)
1989	DE Associate of the Year

National Association of REALTORS®
1991 to present	Publications Committee
1991 to present	Economics Summit
1991 to present	GRI Instructor

National and State Designations
- ☆ Certified Residential Specialist (CRS)
- ☆ Graduate of the Delaware REALTORS® Institute (GRI)
- ☆ Certified Residential Broker Candidate (CRB)

Licenses
Delaware Real Estate License
Maryland Real Estate License
Pennsylvania Real Estate License
Brokers License - 1990

Community Involvement
1990	Instructor in "Broker's Licensing Course," U of DE
1988 to pres.	Director, Delaware Special Olympics
1989	Graduate Leadership Delaware (United Way)

Production
- ☆ Sales and listings 1985 to present of over $45 Million
- ☆ Coauthored *Targeting the Over 55 Client* - a Real Estate agent's guide to today's fastest growing market
- ☆ Dozen Award Recipient 1991, 1992, 1993, 1994 (Top 3% of Salespeople Nationally)
- ☆ Lifetime Member - New Castle County Board of REALTORS® Million Dollar Club

Media
- ☆ WHYY Television News Real Estate Expert
- ☆ Host of WILM News Radio's "Real Estate Talk" since 1987
- ☆ Contributing Writer for Wilmington News Journal's Real Estate column

Now, in my eleventh year of Real Estate Sales I am realizing in excess of ninety percent of my business through past customers and clients or their referrals.

Some of my most noteworthy career achievements include being honored by my peers as State REALTOR® Associate of the Year; coauthoring *Targeting the Over 55 Client* with my wife Betsy and John Tucillo, Chief Economist of NAR; and receiving the National Association of REALTORS® Journalism Award for work on my weekly radio talk show, *Real Estate Talk*, which has since become Delaware's "Voice of Real Estate".

The Right Direction . . . In Real Estate

Prepared by Betsy & Buddy West, CRS's, GRI's
Patterson Schwartz & Assoc., Inc.

Prepared for Tom & Carol Hawley

CALENDAR OF EVENTS
HOW WE WORK

Please let us explain how we will handle the sequence of activities related to the pricing and listing of your home.

THE FIRST VISIT

We begin the process with a visit to your home to gather general information about it and to take measurements of the rooms. We'll be especially interested in features, systems and improvements that you have made. We would also like to know what prompts your decision to move. This visit should take between 30 minutes and an hour, and during that time we will be laying the groundwork for the marketing of this special home . . . so we'll be asking you to think about things that you particularly enjoy in your home and what led you to choose this home over others.

BEHIND THE SCENES

Once we have this information in hand, we can complete a comprehensive profile of the home and add additional details that are available in our office. All comparable homes currently for sale and recently sold are taken from our database as well as similar homes also for sale in your market area. We will complete a detailed market analysis that will reflect market conditions and circumstances at this time. This work generally takes a day or two.

THE SECOND VISIT

Then we will want to have between an hour and two hours to sit with you... to introduce ourselves to you, review the pricing presentation with you, and perhaps most importantly, to answer your questions. The goal of this meeting is to provide you with enough information to make informed decisions regarding the pricing of your home and the choice of your agent(s). This is very much an educational process and may be the most important time that we will spend together.

This pre-listing period is critically important to you because to achieve the sale of your home and maximize net proceeds you must consider five variables: price, terms, condition, location and the choice of agent. Four of these are under your control and, especially in today's market, your choice of agent(s) is the most significant component in a successful sale. Why? Because a good agent will guide you in establishing price, in considering terms, in preparing your home for marketing and be well prepared to represent you and your home proactively!

Prepared by Betsy & Buddy West, CRS's, GRI's
Patterson Schwartz & Assoc., Inc.

Prepared for Tom & Carol Hawley

EXCLUSIVE SERVICES PROVIDED

COMPARATIVE MARKET ANALYSIS

A written report of the transactions in the neighborhood to identify similar properties that have sold recently and are currently on the market in an effort to determine a realistic price for the subject property.

MARKET PREPARATION GUIDE

Helping sellers to think like buyers helps them to understand the importance of preparing their homes for the market. Detailed guidance and step by step assistance is given to ensure that your home stands out in the marketplace.

MARKETING PLAN

A comprehensive marketing plan presented in writing is customized for the seller. Our objectives are: to bring you as many qualified buyers as possible, to communicate the results of our efforts to you regularly, and to assist you in getting the highest possible dollar value for your home with the least amount of complications in the shortest possible time.

MARKETING ACTIVITY & SHOWING REPORTS

If your home is not sold within 30 days of listing you may expect a written progress report within the next two weeks. This recap of marketing activities and composite of feedback from the agents who have shown your home will help us to reassess our selling strategies for the next 30 days. Additionally, you may expect to receive contact by phone at least weekly.

MOVING RESOURCE PACKET

This packet of information will be tailored to you, your moving plans and future needs. These resources are continually updated and additional ideas are always welcome to help the next seller's move to be easier.

RELOCATION PACKAGE

If you are moving to another city a complete portfolio of information can be forwarded to you. This can be very helpful in orienting you to the local housing market as well as schools, shopping, transportation, entertainment, and other areas of specific interest to you.

Prepared by Betsy & Buddy West, CRS's, GRI's
Patterson Schwartz & Assoc., Inc.

Prepared for Tom & Carol Hawley

The Importance of Correct Pricing!

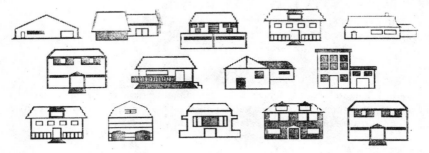

Today, for Every 12 Houses on the Market

There is Only 1 Buyer!

If your home is not competitively priced and in tip top condition, by the process of elimination, yours will be the last to sell and may require more than one substantial price reduction over an extended period of time to arrive at the price the market is willing to pay. Market price for houses, like the market price for all goods and services, is determined by one and only one factor . . .

Supply & Demand!

Source:
New Castle County Board of Realtors

Prepared by Betsy & Buddy West, CRS's, GRI's
Patterson Schwartz & Assoc., Inc.

Prepared for Tom & Carol Hawley

WHAT DETERMINES VALUE?

	YES	NO
Improvements?	☑	☑
What We Say?	☐	☑
What Any Number of Other Realtors Say?	☐	☑
How Much You Need?	☐	☑
Original Purchase Price?	☐	☑
Market Trends (Rising, Falling, Level)?	☑	☐
Actual Neighborhood Sale Prices?	☑	☐
Competition?	☑	☐
Condition of the Property?	☑	☐

Prepared by Betsy & Buddy West, CRS's, GRI's
Patterson Schwartz & Assoc., Inc.

Prepared for Tom & Carol Hawley

Prepared by Betsy & Buddy West, CRS's, GRI's
Patterson Schwartz & Assoc., Inc.

A PRICING PRESENTATION

Prepared especially for

Tom & Carol Hawley
2208 Grand Ave.
Wilmington, DE 19801

Another Personal Service by

Betsy & Buddy West, CRS's, GRI's
Patterson Schwartz & Assoc., Inc.
913 Delaware Ave.
Wilmington, DE 19806
302-429-7372
302-576-9378

Prepared for Tom & Carol Hawley

The seller sets the price of
the home, but ultimately the
buyer determines the value.

Our job is to supply you with
facts about what has sold
recently and what is for sale now
to help you make a decision.

Prepared for Tom & Carol Hawley

Houses sell quickly and usually for the most money when they are priced properly in the beginning.

Prepared by Betsy & Buddy West, CRS's, GRI's
Patterson Schwartz & Assoc., Inc.

Prepared for Tom & Carol Hawley

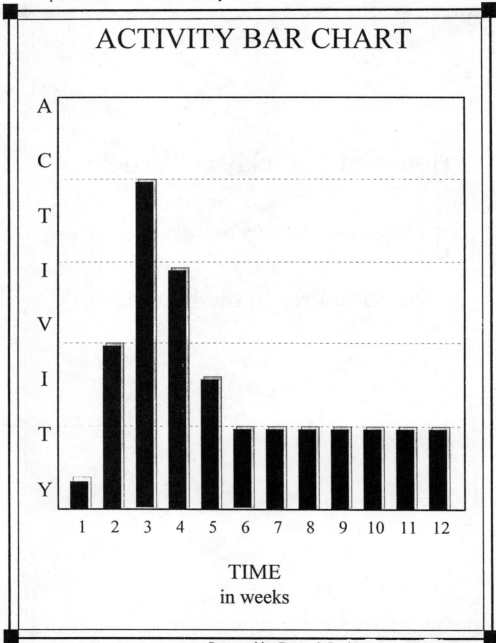

ACTIVITY BAR CHART

TIME
in weeks

Prepared by Betsy & Buddy West, CRS's, GRI's
Patterson Schwartz & Assoc., Inc.

Prepared for Tom & Carol Hawley

Average Difference Between List Price and Selling Price by Length of Time on Market

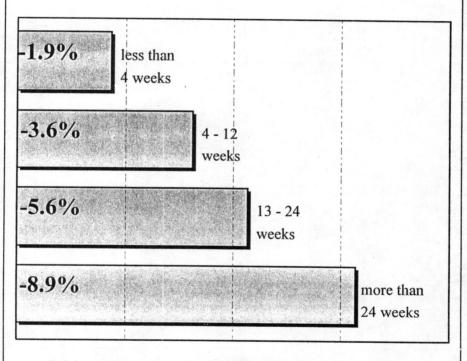

Pricing your home correctly in the beginning will net you more!

Based on NAR Homebuying & Selling Survey.

Prepared by Betsy & Buddy West, CRS's, GRI's
Patterson Schwartz & Assoc., Inc.

Comparative Market Analysis
SOLD PROPERTIES

Prepared for:

Tom & Carol Hawley

2208 Grand Ave.

Wilmington, DE 19801

Prepared by:

Betsy & Buddy West, CRS's, GRI's

Patterson Schwartz & Assoc., Inc.

913 Delaware Ave.

Wilmington, DE 19806

	SUBJECT 2208 Grand Ave.	COMP #1 2402 West 17th St.	COMP #2 2506 Willard St.	COMP #3 7 Red Oak Rd.
Proximity		.5 mi.	.5 mi	.5 mi
Date Sold		10/31/94	2/6/94	9/26/94
Sales Price		515,000	500,000	570,000
Sq. Footage	3500	3000	2800	3500
Lot Size	260 x 150	145 x 150	206 x 117	165 x 128
Age	75	83	Unknown	90
Condition	Fair	Good	Fair/Good	Good
# of Bedrooms	5	6	5	8
# of Baths	5	4.5	3.5	5.5+
Garage	2 Car - Tandem	2 Car	2 Car & Carport	No-Off Street
Basement	Yes-Part Above Grn	Yes	Yes	Yes
Heating & A/C	OHW / Units	GHA / C/A - 2nd Fl	GHA / C/A	Unknown/Units
Fireplaces	3	4	3	4
Family Room	Yes & Den	Yes & Den	Yes & Den-2nd Flr	Yes & Den - 2nd Flr

Marketing Pluses: Location and setting are very attractive and protected from the traffic of some of the comparables. Home is more formal than some and well designed.

Marketing Minuses: Condition is fair with some deferred maintenance that detracts from the expectations of those in this price range and raises questions of dollars to be spent to bring it up to "move-in."

Subject Property
Indicated Price Range: $475,000-490,000

Suggested
List Price: $495,000

Prepared for Tom & Carol Hawley

PRICING TO SELL
The Importance of the One Hundred Thousand Dollar Barrier

—

01%   **$524,900**

—————

—————

30%   **$499,900**

———————

———————

50%   **$490,000**

—————————

—————————

75%   **$480,000**

———————————

———————————

99%   **$449,000**

—————————————

Available, qualified, interested buyers looking at your home.

How much of the market
do you want to attract?

Prepared by Betsy & Buddy West, CRS's, GRI's
Patterson Schwartz & Assoc., Inc.

Seller's Estimated
Closing Costs

Patterson Schwartz
REAL ESTATE

Address of Property _____

Selling Price $ _____   Today's Date _____

Reductions in Amount Due to Seller

    1st Mortgage Balance   _____
       Current Month's Interest   _____
    2nd Mortgage Balance   _____
       Current Month's Interest   _____
    Other Liens   _____
    Pre-Payment Penalty   _____

          Sub Total   _____ _____

Closing Costs

    Real Estate Commission   _____
    Transfer Tax   _____
    Wood-Destroying Insect Infestation Report   _____
    Wood-Destorying Insect Treatment and/or Repair   _____
    Mortgage Satisfaction Fee   _____
    Overnight Mail Charges (mortgage pay-off)   _____
    Homeowner's Warranty   _____
    Unpaid Taxes, Water, Sewer, Other Lienable Charges   _____

          Sub Total   _____ _____

Payments Made on Buyer's Behalf   _____

    Points   _____
    Settlement   _____
    Lender's Miscellaneous Charges   _____
    Estimated Repairs (FHA/VA)   _____
    Inspection Fees (FHA/VA)   _____
    Reinspection Fees (FHA/VA)

          Sub Total   _____ _____

          Total Estimated Closing Costs   _____

Selling Price   _____

Estimated Closing Costs   —   _____

Seller's Estimated Net (plus prorations and escrows)   _____

Form No. 003, Rev. 5/93

HOMEOWNER'S HOMEWORK

Please help us:

1.   Review your property description. Advise Betsy of any omissions or corrections.

2.   We will need the following:

     _____ A copy of your deed.

     _____ A key(s) for your house.

     _____ A survey of your property if you have one.

     _____ Name / address / phone # of your mortgage company & loan account #.

     _____ Your social security number(s).

     _____ Your choice of termite company.

     _____ Other. _____ _____

3.   Other things to be done:

     _____ Do you have a working smoke detector on each level of your home?

RECORD OF SHOWINGS

As convenient, please call Betsy's office to advise of showings. It's fine to leave a message with the information noted below.
If you have cards with the agent's office phone number, that would be helpful too.
429-7348

DATE/TIME OF SHOWING	AGENT SHOWING	AGENT'S COMPANY	BUYER'S AGENT?

30 DAY MARKETING PLAN

The following is our plan for marketing your home:

WEEK ONE:

_____ Prepare a written comparative market analysis
_____ Present Marketing Plan
_____ Place your home in PSA Listing Management System
_____ Submit your home to appropriate multilist systems
_____ Install sign and lockbox
_____ Take pictures
_____ Place property description information in your home
_____ Provide mortgage information sheets
_____ Write/submit classified ad
_____ Write/submit/check "Hotline" ad (Please review, 234-5200)
_____ Check multilist information for accuracy - Attached
_____ Determine and solicit target market for your home
_____ Call 10 agents to tell them about your home
_____ Schedule office tour - Approx. 30 Wilmington PSA agents
_____ Develop and deliver custom brochures
_____ Prepare custom promotional flier and distribute to target
       agents & others

WEEK TWO:

_____ Provide home & community information booklet
_____ Special feature frames/Check with sellers, Do they Wish?
_____ Schedule open house/Deliver open house announcements
_____ Send "thank yous" to open house visitors
_____ Review results and feedback from open house with you

WEEK THREE:

_____ Replenish sheets/Check sign condition/Update listing information
_____ Special promotions/Report on showing feedback (reg and monthly)
_____ Written report updating market activity after 30 days
_____ Place SOLD sign on property

Prepared for Tom & Carol Hawley

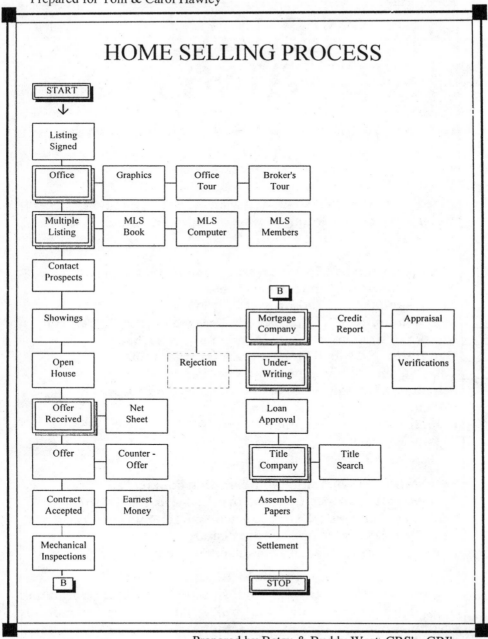

HOME SELLING PROCESS

Prepared by Betsy & Buddy West, CRS's, GRI's
Patterson Schwartz & Assoc., Inc.

WHAT TO EXPECT

THE FIRST DAYS AND WEEKS

Your home will be entered into the computer within 24-48 hours after it has been listed. This means that the information on your home will be immediately available to any agent that is in our Multiple Listing Service. If an agent is actively searching for a new listing with special features that your home has, then it is conceivable that your home will be shown within a few days after it has been listed. However, sometimes things get started slowly, depending upon the time of year and number of competing homes for sale.

We use this first week to: bring the Property Descriptions and Seller's Disclosure Forms to you home, fine tune the showing procedure for your home, get your For Sale sign installed with Hotline number, and work on the upcoming marketing activities including brochures and other promotional materials.

Please be sure that the information on the Property Description and any other materials that I may prepare on your home is correct. Usually I'll see that you have a draft to review, but please check my work! This information should be out for the agents and prospective buyers to take. Just let me know if supplies of any materials run low and I'll take care of re-filling them.

ABOUT OFFICE TOURS

Our office tours new listings on Tuesdays after our sales meeting generally between 10:00 and 12:00. This is when the agents from our office walk through your home. Homes are usually toured within the first month of the listing. Because of the large number of homes on the market, we travel to different geographical areas weekly. If we have just been in your area , it could be a little longer.

We will notify you no later than the Monday before. If you are home when the tour comes through, it may appear that the agents "fly through" your home, but they are there just to become acquainted with the layout and the showing condition of the home. Please don't consider it an insult. When showing it to a buyer, they obviously will spend more time.

Important - Please have your home ready for the tour the same way you would if a buyer is coming. Have it picked up, the lights and music on, the pets out of the way and the potpourri out! The agent's first impression is as important as the buyer's.

ABOUT APPOINTMENTS: HOW APPOINTMENTS ARE MADE

Many of the calls for appointments to show your home will come via our Appointment Center. Schedulers there take care of making arrangements for showings for all agents from other companies as well as Patterson Schwartz agents. Patterson Schwartz agents may also call you directly to set a time. Please try to make a note of the agent showing your home, his or her company and the time of the showing. You'll have a log to record this information. At your convenience please call Betsy's office (429-7348) and pass it along to her so that she can follow up with agent who will or has shown your home.

BEING ON TIME FOR APPOINTMENTS

It is important to understand why sometimes agents can't be at your home in the time frame that they have requested. Sometimes the buyer is late for the appointment, or they stay longer at one or more houses throwing the agent's schedule off. Some people look at houses in five minutes, while some Libras like Betsy may take 20 minutes. We often have no way of knowing this so it can throw our schedule off. Your understanding of this is appreciated.

NO SHOWS

Sometimes a buyer changes direction on us in mid-stream with what they want to look at so an agent has to go to entirely different areas or subdivisions, and may not be able to call you at that moment to cancel the appointment. Or, sometimes they might try to call and you're not at home. We apologize for the inconvenience if this should happen. It is not commonplace, but if it does occur please let us know so that we can try to find out the reason why.

ARRIVING ON
SHORT NOTICE OR
WITHOUT AN APPOINTMENT

Occasionally, especially with easy access by car phone, agents may call on short notice to show your home. They may even come to the front door and knock if they are driving through the neighborhood with a customer. If at all possible, please allow them to come in...just ask them to give you five minutes to "tidy up". A little clutter, or preparation of a meal in the kitchen will not prevent your home from selling. Take the five minutes, turn on the lights and put away anything that could be extremely distracting. Tell the agent that he or she can walk around the outside of the house while you are getting ready.

WHAT TO DO WHILE BUYERS
ARE LOOKING

It is not necessary for you to leave home every time an agent makes an appointment, but when they do arrive, take a walk outside, or if the weather does not permit, go to one corner of the house out of "earshot" so that the buyer feels comfortable in making comments about your home to their agent. Be cautious in talking to the customer - the one thing you may want pointed out about your home may be the one thing the buyer

isn't too keen about! Casual remarks that you feel are harmless could possibly cause the prospect to eliminate your home. Remember, though neither the agent nor the buyer knows your home as well you do, the salesperson does know the buyer.

A note about valuables - put them away, especially small things like jewelry. We have had no problems in this regard, but make it a practice not to invite trouble.

KEEPING ON TOP
OF CONDITION

Just like any other showroom, your home needs to appear in "perfect" condition every day! That's difficult and we understand. But a home remaining unsold on the market is more trouble than keeping it tidy in the short term. Condition is one important way in which a seller says, "I care" and that's very important to most buyers.

Setting the stage and mood really does help a house to sell. If you have dark room or dark halls, leave a light on all the time. Otherwise, just turn some lights on in anticipation of a showing. If it's hot outside turn on the air conditioning and if it's cold outside make sure your home is warm inside. Things that smell good like baking cookies or a low key potpourri are good. Other smells like pets, cigarettes and mustiness should be eliminated if at all possible.

FEEDBACK
AND FOLLOW-UP

As mentioned earlier your calls to report showings and the reports sent to us from the appointment center will allow me to follow-up with agents who have showed your home. Sometimes it takes several tries and several days to reach agents. If there is something of importance to share with you about the showing I will always reach you quickly. Otherwise, the comments will be compiled in an activity tracking report that you will receive at approximately 30 day intervals. Of course, I will be in touch with you by phone on a weekly basis and you may always feel free to call me. When possible please call my office number - 429-7348.

Marketing Service Report
Page 1

Prepared for Tom & Carol Hawley
2208 Grand Avenue

Prepared by

Described below is an overview of the showing activities over the past several weeks.

Date \ Activity		Description
11/15/94	Showing-L. Zurkow/PSA	Preview of market for banker from Phila. area.
11/18/94	Showing-E. Schwartz/PS	(L) Wife and extended family looking. Some concerns about floor plan for family needs. Degree of motivation?
11/19/94	Showing-G. Saffer/PSA	(L) Wife with agent. Has been looking for some time. Did not appear particularly serious.
11/20/94	Brokers Open House	Approximately 30 sales people attended. Purpose to introduce the home to agents and extend the network of opportunity for showings.
11/30/94	Showing-W.Bunch/REMAX	(T) These buyers have been renting locally. Are now ready to buy, but not sure between older home and new construction.
12/01/94	Showing-K.Pigliacampli	(L) Buyers have sold home in Somerset Lake. Looking to move up. May be beyond financial comfort level of this couple. Bought Kennett Pike in $500,000 range.
12/05/94	Showing-A.Wilson/PPP	(T) Leaning to less formal, more contemporary.
12/05/94	Showing-S. Witsil/WITS	(L) Required too much renovation at the price for this buyer.
12/10/94	Inquiry-B.Ortner/PSA	(T) Buyer has not yet accepted job. Based on her preview feels he is leaning to new construction to get floor plan for family, in-laws and help. Liked Way Ridge.

Showing activity has been good. General feedback indicates that the home may be too formal for the lifestyles of some of the prospective buyers. Additionally, the close-ended kitchen has been a concern expressed and at the listing price no one has been willing to undertake renovations to the house.

PUTTING YOUR HOME TO THE TEST

INSPECTIONS

There are a number of possible inspections of the property that may be called for in the sales contract. Sometimes, sellers have certain inspections completed before their home is even listed for sale. Inspection clauses in a sales contract permit a buyer to hire a professional inspector to examine the property. If there are conditions that are unsatisfactory to the buyer, the buyer may request the seller to repair the condition. If the request is denied, the buyer may elect to cancel the contract. More often, depending upon the repair required, the cost to correct is negotiated between buyer and seller. Usually inspections are completed within a week or so from the signing of the contract and another several days are allowed for the parties to decide what they will do if a concern has been raised. Also there may be a dollar limit noted under which a found deficiency may not qualify for repair by the seller. This helps eliminate small items from the "fix-it" list.

A HOME INSPECTION

This is the most common of "optional" inspections called for in our sales contracts. Most REALTORS® now recommend that home buyers obtain a professional home inspection. This inspection benefits both the buyer and the seller. The buyer knows that a trained expert has inspected the most costly repair items in the home. The seller can move on knowing that the buyer accepts the condition of the property based on expert advice. The buyer will pay in the range of $250.00 for this evaluation.

The inspection is very thorough and takes about two hours to complete. The inspector usually starts on the outside of the house and works his way through the inside from top to bottom. Items covered include the roof, basement, heating, plumbing and electrical systems, kitchen appliances and overall structural soundness. A detailed written report is given to the buyer with comments on any items found to be defective.

Very rarely is a condition revealed that cannot be remedied. Just as important as the possible discovery of a defect in the property, the home inspection serves to introduce the buyer to the "underpinnings" his new home and help him to know what kinds of future maintenance may be required. Education is a significant benefit of the home inspection.

A RADON INSPECTION

You cannot see radon nor can you smell or taste it. It is a potentially cancer causing radioactive gas found in the earth's rock and soil. It is formed by the natural breakdown of radium (a decay product of uranium). It typically moves up through the ground to the air above and into your home through the following: cracks in solid floors, construction joints, cracks in walls, gaps in suspended floors, gaps around pipes, cavities inside walls or the water supply if you have a well. Nearly one out of every 15 homes in the U.S. is estimated to have elevated radon levels, and while radon problems may be more common in some areas, any home may be at risk. The only way to know for sure is to test.

Sellers may decide to do a radon test before putting their home on the market or they may wait until the prospective buyer requests one. When the monitoring unit is in place for the test it is important to keep windows and outside doors closed as much as possible, except for normal entry and exit.

If the test reveals a radon level 4 picocuries per liter or higher (a standard set by the EPA) then a second test will likely be conducted. If the level remains high it will be necessary to take action to reduce the radon level. The type of remediation, as it is sometimes called, will depend upon the design of the home and other factors. It may involve a combination of sealing entry points and increasing air circulation.

THE TERMITE INSPECTION

A Wood Destroying Insect Infestation Report is a required part of our sales contract. This report is commonly referred to as the termite report because the Subterranean termite is the number one wood destroying pest in the U.S. In our area it has been said that there are only two types of houses, "those that have termites and those that will." Additionally, this inspection also checks for certain kinds of beetles, carpenter ants and wood rot. All of these, left unchecked, can cause extensive damage, sometimes of a structural nature, to a home. For this reason a prospective buyer and his mortgage company need to be assured that there is no evidence of active infestation or structural damage from an infestation.

Our contracts call for the seller to choose a termite company and to pay for the inspection. If you are under contract with a termite company they *may* agree to

conduct the inspection at a reduced rate. The inspection for the purposes of a transfer of property must be done within a certain specific time frame depending upon the buyers' lender and the date of settlement. We will coordinate the timing with you. If an active infestation is discovered, you will be responsible for having it treated. If you elect not to have the infestation treated, the buyer may decline to take the house.

If as a result of either active or past infestation there is any evidence of damage *at all* it will likely necessitate having that damage examined by a licensed contractor. If there is evidence of structural damage it will need to be repaired. This cost is usually borne by the seller.

WELL WATER AND SEPTIC SYSTEMS

If you have a well and/or a septic system it will be checked by the buyer's inspector. It is recommended that a seller have their septic system pumped every three years and before the septic inspections are done. Various tests will be done to check to quality of well water. The standard tests are: Coliform; pH; Iron; Manganese; Hardness; and Nitrates. When the test results exceed the Board of Health standards, the seller will be required to correct the problem.

ASBESTOS, BURIED FUEL TANKS AND LEAD PAINT

These are red flags and potential buyers may be reluctant to consider a property until these kinds of problems are addressed. What course of action may be necessary depends upon the specific circumstances. It is your responsibility to begin by acknowledging the presence of any of these items.

GLITCHES

Sometimes, despite our best intentions and efforts, small snags present themselves at close to the 11th hour of the transaction. Of course it won't be every one of the glitches described here and usually it won't be any of them. However, while we may not be able to avoid every one, understanding: what might happen, why it could happen and what you need to do to remedy the problem is the way to get on with your move.

In Delaware the buyers of homes engage an attorney to: do the title search, coordinate details of the settlement and conduct the settlement. There is usually no reason for the seller to involve an attorney and the need to address the kinds of issues described here would not change if you did hire one to represent your interests.

The work that the attorney oversees and authorizes involves expenditure of funds, usually the buyers, and is therefore not undertaken until the buyer has been approved for a mortgage, usually a couple of weeks before the settlement date. The following have been known to occur:

PAID OFF MORTGAGES

The sellers' mortgage has been paid in full, but the mortgage document has not been marked satisfied of record in the Recorder of Deeds office. When the mortgage is paid off, the mortgage company usually sends the original note and mortgage marked paid in full and a power of attorney which should be recorded in the Recorder of Deeds office to satisfy the mortgage of record. Often the homeowner receiving these documents does not realize that the power of attorney must be recorded.

When the buyer's attorney does the title search, the mortgage then shows up as being open of record. It is the seller's responsibility to remove this old lien against the property. This may cause considerable stress on the seller just prior to the closing. Also there will be an extra charge to the seller by the attorney to do the leg work to find out what happened and to get the necessary paperwork from the mortgage company to satisfy the mortgage. This 11th hour flurry of activity can be avoided if the seller has a lien search done on the property at the time of listing the home.

DEATH OF A FORMER OWNER

In the course of searching the title the attorney finds more names on the last recorded deed than appear on the sellers's side of the current sales contract. In that case there must be an explanation for the omission of the name(s). In the case of a former owner's death, before the property can be transferred, documents must be filed in the Register of Wills Office in the County where the property is located to establish of record that the person has died and that his or her interest in the property has passed to the surviving spouse.

Local laws will also determine whether a formal estate must be opened or not. This must be done to establish "chain of title". The chain of title is the link from one owner of the property to the next. If a deed to the property went to two people, the deed transferring the property to subsequent owners must also be signed by the same two people. If one of them has died, the official records must contain the necessary documents to establish that the person has died and that no estate taxes are owed. Sometimes when one of the original owners of a property has died many years ago and the property was held as tenants by the entirety with the right of survivorship, the surviving spouse did nothing with the estate. All of their property was owned jointly and everthing automatically went to the surviving spouse. However, to establish the chain of title, other documents must be filed. At the time of listing the property, the seller should consult an attorney to have him examine the deed and look at local laws to see if the necessary documents have been filed of record to establish the chain of title.

ENCROACHMENTS

When the survey of your property is completed something, often a storage shed or driveway, belonging to your property is found to be sitting on a neighbor's land, or vice versa. When this is the case the company providing title insurance to the new buyer or his lender will not do so until: the offending encroachment is moved or the adjoining neighbor gives his written okay for the condition to continue. The specifics of the encroachment dictate which course of action we will take.

FINAL FIGURES & CHARGES

A compilation of your final figures from the attorney's office is usually not available until the day before or even the day of the settlement. We try to get those final figures to review with you whenever possible. Sometimes an unanticipated charge appears that must be looked into and resolved. Unanticipated is the key word. We will get to the bottom of it.

TERMITE TROUBLE

Though you may be under contract with a termite company, the sales contract is very specific about the time frame for completing the "wood destroying insect infestation" report. If an infestation is discovered it must be treated and if there is any evidence of damage due to either a current infestation or a previous infestation we need to arrange for a licensed contractor to inspect the damaged area. You will be responsible for paying the contractor. This all could unfold in the final weeks prior to settlement.

A PRESETTLEMENT INSPECTION PROBLEM

Forty eight hours prior to settlement your buyer has the right to walk through your house to do a presettlement inspection. He is confirming that the condition of your home is the same now as it was when the offer was made and accepted. He is also confirming that the agreed upon inclusions and exclusions are in place or gone. Additionally, by the terms of most contracts the buyer is expecting that the systems- things like heating/cooling, electrical, appliances- are in working order unless noted previously. Buyers understand that depending upon the time of their walk through all of the moving out may not be finished. Sellers understand that their home must be completely empty and broom swept clean at the time of settlement. A note - the removal of unwanted household goods and trash may involve some expense and planning. It is your responsibility to take care of such disposal. We have resource information for you.

Sometimes in the course of the pre-settlement inspection the buyer discovers a problem. Most of the time they're small problems often as a result of miscommunication. We talk them through and find a resolution. Occasionally, when both parties are unwilling to give beyond a certain point or when the problem is discovered very late, we must wait until we sit at the settlement table to reach a resolve. Be assured, we always find a solution and 99% of the time both seller and buyer find it an acceptable one.

Okay, we can't think of any other glitches right now. Every settlement brings something new. Our responsibility is to anticipate and head off potential problems whenever possible, to help you to understand why certain conditions must be met and to help you to arrange to meet those conditions. We are here to help you both behind the scenes and in the resolution of the unanticipated. We often do some of our best work in the final days before settlement!

SELLER'S CHECK LIST

☐ Notify your mortgagee immediately in writing that your house has been sold and you will pay off your mortgage loan.
☐ Gather your receipted bills for taxes, water, sewer and civic association dues/fees.
☐ Notify utilities when to read your meters:

New Castle County
Delmarva Power, 302-454-0313
Newark Electric & Water, 302-366-7085
Wilmington City Water, 302-571-4320
Wilmington Suburban Water, 302-633-5900
Artisian Water, 302-453-6930

Pennsylvania
Peco Energy, 610-384-3000
Water, call township for supplier

Maryland
Conowingo Power, 410-398-1400
Water, call municipality for supplier

☐ Notify telephone company:
Delaware: Bell Atlantic of Delaware,
302-421-5000 or 1-800-942-5000
Pennsylvania: Bell Atlantic of Pennsylvania,
610-590-6200 or 1-800-640-4155
Maryland: C&P Telephone,
410-954-6230

☐ Notify cable television company- TCI Cablevision, 302-656-3370
☐ Cancel any regular deliveries, i.e. newspaper.
☐ Notify your fuel dealer and obtain oil reading.
☐ Notify garbage/trash remover.
☐ Notify your mover.
☐ Send change of address cards (available from us).
☐ After settlement, cancel or transfer fire and/or homeowner's insurance.
☐ Put all appliance/houshold equipment info in a kitchen cabinet drawer.
☐ Remove all personal belongings from home.
☐ Have home "broom swept clean".
☐ Bring all keys and electric garage door openers to settlement.

If your home will be vacant:
☐ Notify police.
☐ Arrange for lawn care or snow removal.
☐ "Winterize" house if necessary

MOVING LIST

Patterson Schwartz

R E A L   E S T A T E

Things to do before and after you move.

Before You Leave:

❑ Read gas, electric and water meters.
❑ Notify telephone company.
❑ Cancel regular deliveries, i.e. newspapers.
❑ Have refrigerator and other appliances serviced for trip.
❑ Write to utility company in city to which you are moving and ask about necessary fees or deposits.
❑ Send your forwarding address to your local post office; send change of address cards to publications, insurance companies, etc.
❑ Transfer your insurance on personal possessions so they will be covered at your new home and en route.
❑ Notify your place of worship you are leaving.
❑ Arrange to get medical records, prescriptions, etc.
❑ If car or other possessions are not paid for, get permission to move them.
❑ Have your present bank arrange credit references for establishing new accounts if moving to a new city.
❑ Leave a set of keys to your old property with agent or neighbor.

After You Arrive:

❑ Check on service of telephone, gas, electricity, water, etc.
❑ Have stove serviced and check any pilot lights.
❑ Have refrigerator, washer, dryer checked.
❑ Ask letter carrier for mail he or she may be holding for your arrival.
❑ Register for voting.
❑ Register car within five days after arrival in new state or penalty may have to be paid.
❑ Change address on driver's license or obtain new license.
❑ Open new bank accounts.

Appendix A
State Agencies on Housing and Aging

Alabama

Aging Commission
770 Washington Ave., Suite 470
Montgomery, AL 36130
205-242-5743

Housing Finance Authority
PO Box 230909
Montgomery, AL 36123-0909
205-244-9200

American Samoa

Aging Administration
Office of the Governor
Pago Pago, American Samoa 96799
684-633-1251

Alaska

Housing Finance Corporation
PO Box 101020
Anchorage, AK 99510-1020
907-561-1900

Arizona

Aging and Adult Administration
Economic Security Department
PO Box 6123
Phoenix, AZ 85005
602-542-4446

Housing Finance Review Board
3800 N. Central Ave., Suite 1200
Phoenix, AZ 85012
602-280-1365

Arkansas

Aging & Adult Services Division
Human Services Department
PO Box 1437
Little Rock, AR 72203
501-682-8521

Development Finance Authority
PO Box 8023
Little Rock, AR 72203
501-682-5900

California

Aging Commission
1020 9th Street., Room 260
Sacramento, CA 95814
916-322-5630

Housing Finance Agency
1121 L Street, 7th floor
Sacramento, CA 95814
916-322-3991

Colorado

Commission for Aging
Social Services Department
1575 Sherman Street
Denver, CO 80203-1714
303-866-3851

Housing Division
Local Affairs Department
1313 Sherman Street, Room 518
Denver, CO 80203
303-866-2033

Connecticut

Elderly Services Division
25 Sigourney Street
Hartford, CT 06106
203-424-5274

Housing Department
505 Hudson Street
Hartford, CT 06106-7106
203-566-8415

Delaware

Aging Division
Health & Social Services
    Department
1901 North Dupont Hiway
New Castle, DE 19720
302-577-4660

Housing Authority
18 The Green
Dover, DE 19901
302-739-4263

District of Columbia

Aging Office
1424 K Street, NW, 2nd Floor
Washington, DC 20005
202-724-5622

Housing and Community
    Development Department
51 N Street, NE
Washington, DC 20002
202-535-1970

Florida

Aging & Adult Services Office
Health and Rehabilitative Services
    Department
1317 Winewood Boulevard
Tallahassee, FL 32399-0700
904-488-8922

Housing & Community
    Development Division
Community Affairs Department
2740 Centerview Drive
Tallahassee, FL 32399-2100
904-488-7956

Georgia

Aging Services Office
2 Peachtree Street, NW
Atlanta, GA 30303
404-894-2023

Residential Finance Authority
60 Executive Park South, NE,
    Suite 250
Atlanta, GA 30329
404-679-4840

Guam

Housing and Urban Renewal
   Authority
Office of the Governor
PO Box CS
Agana, GU 96910
671-477-9851

Hawaii

Aging Office
335 Merchant Street, Room 241
Honolulu, HI 96813
808-586-0100

Housing Authority
1002 N School Street
Honolulu, HI 96817
808-832-6020

Idaho

Aging Office
PO Box 83720
Boise, ID 83720-0007
208-334-3833

Housing Agency
PO Box 7899
Boise, ID 83707-1899
208-331-4882

Illinois

Aging Department
421 East Capitol Ave., #100
Springfield, IL 62701-1789
217-785-2870

Community Development Bureau
Commerce and Community Affairs
   Department
620 East Adams
Springfield, IL 62701
217-782-6136

Indiana

Aging & Rehabilitative Services
  Division
Family and Social Services
  Administration
402 West Washington Street,
  Room W341
Indianapolis, IN 46204
317-232-1147

Housing Units
Family and Social Services
  Administration
402 West Washington Street,
  Room W341
Indianapolis, IN 46204
317-232-7045

Iowa

Elder Affairs Department
236 Jewett Building
914 Grand Avenue
Des Moines, IA 50309
515-281-5188

Housing & Community Bureau
Economic Development
  Department
200 East Grand Avenue
Des Moines, IA 50309
515-242-4837

Kansas

Aging Department
915 SW Harrison Street, Room 150
Topeka, KS 66612-1500
913-296-4986

Housing Under Secretary
Commerce and Housing
  Department
700 SW Harrison Street, Suite 1300
Topeka, KS 66603-3712
913-296-2686

Kentucky

Aging Services Division
Social Services Department
275 E Main Street
Frankfort, KY 40621
502-562-6930

Housing Corporation
1231 Louisville, Road
Frankfort, KY 40601
502-564-7630

Maine

Elder & Adult Services Bureau
Human Services Department
State House, Station 11
Augusta, ME 04333
207-624-5335

Housing Authority
PO Box 2669
Augusta, ME 04338-2669
207-626-4600

Maryland

Aging Office
301 West Preston Street,
   Room 1004
Baltimore, MD 21201-2374
410-225-1102

Housing and Community
   Development Department
100 Community Place
Crownsville, MD 21032-2023
410-514-7005

Massachusetts

Elder Affairs Department
1 Ashburton Place, 5th Floor
Boston, MA 02108
617-727-7750

Administrator
Housing and Community
   Development
100 Cambridge Street, Room 1702
Boston, MA 02202
617-727-7130

Michigan

Aging Office
PO Box 30026
Lansing, MI 48909
517-373-8230

State Housing Development
   Authority
401 South Washington Square,
   Box 30044
Lansing, MI 48909
517-373-6022

Minnesota

Aging Program Division
Social Services Administration
444 Lafayette Road
St. Paul, MN 55155
612-296-2544

Commissioner
Housing Finance Agency
400 Sibley Street, Suite 300
St. Paul, MN 55101
612-296-5738

Mississippi

Aging & Adult Services Division
Human Services Department
PO Box 352
Jackson, MS 39205-0352
601-359-4480

Home Corporation
840 East River Place, Suite 605
Jackson, MS 39202
601-354-6062

Missouri

Aging Division
PO Box 1337
0615 Howerton Court
Jefferson City, MO 65109
314-752-8535

Housing Development
Commission
3770 Broadway
Kansas City, MO 64111
816-756-3790

Montana

Aging Services Coordinator
Family Services Department
Box 8005
Helena, MT 59604
406-444-5900

Board of Housing Division
Commerce Department
1424 9th Avenue
Helena, MT 59620-0501
406-444-3040

Nebraska

Aging Department
PO Box 95044
Lincoln, NE 68509
402-471-2306

Investment Finance Authority
1033 O Street, Suite 218
Lincoln, NE 68508
402-434-8900

Nevada

Aging Services Division
Human Resources Department
505 East King Street, Room 600
Carson City, NV 89710
702-386-3545

Administrator
Housing Division
1802 N Carson Street, Suite 154
Carson City, NV 89710
702-687-4258

New Hampshire

Elderly and Adult Services Division
115 Pleasant Street,
   Annex Building 1
Concord, NH 03301-3843
603-271-4394

Housing Finance Authority
PO Box 5087
Manchester, NH 03108
603-472-8623

New Jersey

Aging Division
Community Affairs Department
CN 800, 101 South Broad Street
Trenton, NJ 08625-0800
609-292-4833

Housing & Development Division
Community Affairs Department
CN 800, 101 South Broad Street
Trenton, NJ 08625-0800
609-633-6246

New Mexico

State Agency on Aging
224 East Palace Avenue
Santa Fe, NM 87501
505-827-7640

State Housing Division
Economic Development
   Department
1100 St. Francis Drive
Santa Fe, NM 87503
505-827-7124

New York

Aging Office
Building 2, Empire State Plaza
Albany, NY 12223-0001
518-474-4425

Commissioner
Housing and Community Renewal
  Division
1 Fordham Plaza
Bronx, NY 10458
718-563-5800

North Carolina

Aging Division
Human Resources Department
1985 Umstead Drive
Raleigh, NC 27603
919-733-3983

Housing Finance Agency
3801 Lake Loon Trail
Raleigh, NC 27611-8066
919-781-6115

North Dakota

Aging Services Division
Human Services Department
600 East Boulevard
Bismarck, ND 58505
701-328-2577

Housing Finance Agency
PO Box 1535
Bismarck, ND 58502-1535
701-328-3434

Ohio

Aging Department
50 West Broad Street, 9th Floor
Columbus, OH 43215-5928
614-466-7246

Housing Finance Agency
77 S. High Street, 26th Floor
Columbus, OH 43266-0314
614-466-7970

Oklahoma

Aging Services Division
Human Services Department
PO Box 25352
Oklahoma City, OK 73125
405-521-2327

Housing Finance Agency
1140 NW 63rd Street, Suite 200
Oklahoma City, OK 73116
405-848-1144

Oregon

Senior and Disabled Services
   Division
500 Summer Street, NE
Salem, OR 97310-1015
503-943-5811

Housing and Community Services
   Department
1600 State Street
Salem, OR 97310-0302
503-986-2000

Pennsylvania

Aging Department
400 Market Street
Harrisburg, PA 17101-2301
717-783-1550

Housing Finance Agency
PO Box 8029
Harrisburg, PA 17105
717-780-3911

Rhode Island

Elderly Affairs Department
160 Pine Street
Providence, RI 02903
401-277-2894

Housing, Energy and Intergovern-
   mental Relations Office
State House, Room 112
Providence, RI 02903-5872
401-277-285

South Carolina

Aging Division
Office of the Governor
2221 Devine Street, Suite 500
Columbia, SC 29205-2471
803-737-7500

Housing Finance and Development
   Authority
919 Bluff Road
Columbia, SC 29201
803-734-2000

South Dakota

Adult Services on Aging office
Social Services Department
700 Governors Drive
Pierre, SD 57501
605-773-3656

Housing Development Authority
221 South Central, PO Box 1237
Pierre, SD 57501-1237
605-773-3181

Tennessee

Aging Commission
706 Church Street, Suite 201
Nashville, TN 37243-0860
615-741-2056

Housing Development Agency
404 James Robertson Parkway
   Suite 1114
Nashville, TN 37243-0900
615-741-2473

Texas

Aging Department
Box 12786
Austin, TX 78711
512-444-2727

Housing and Community Affairs
   Department
PO Box 13941
Austin, TX 78711-3941
512-475-3934

Utah

Aging & Adult Services Division
Human Services Department
PO Box 45500
Salt Lake City, UT 84145-0500
801-538-3910

Community Development Division
Community and Economic
   Development Department
324 South State Street
Salt Lake City, UT 84111
801-538-8700

Vermont

Central Vermont Council on Aging
18 South Main Street
Barre, VT 05641-4697
802-479-0531

Commissioner
Housing and Community Affairs
   Department
Pavillion Office Building
Montpelier, VT 05609-0501
802-828-3217

Virgin Islands

Housing, Parks & Recreation
   Department
Office of the Governor
Kogens Glade
St. Thomas, VI 00802
809-775-0255

Virginia

Commissioner
Aging Department
700 East Franklin Street, 10th Floor
Richmond, VA 23219-2327
804-225-2271

Housing Division
Housing and Community
   Development Department
Jackson Center, 501 N 2nd Street
Richmond, VA 23219-1321
804-371-7100

Washington

Aging and Adult Services
PO Box 45040
Olympia, WA 98504-5040
206-753-3768

Housing Division
Community, Trade and Economic
   Development Department
PO Box 48300
Olympia, WA 98504-8300
206-753-2570

West Virginia

Aging Commission
1900 Kanawha Boulevard
State Capitol Complex
Charleston, WV 25305
304-558-3317

Housing Development Fund
814 Virginia Street, E
Charleston, WV 25301
304-345-6475

Wisconsin

Aging and Long-term Care Board
214 North Hamilton Street
Madison, WI 53703
608-266-8944

Housing and Economic
  Development Authority
PO Box 1728
Madison, WI 53701-1728
608-266-7884

Wyoming

Economic Development &
  Stabilization Division
Commerce Department
Barrett Building
2301 Central Avenue
Cheyenne, WY 82002
307-777-7284

Appendix B
State Housing Finance Authorities

Arkansas Development Finance Authority (ADFA)

NAME OF PROGRAM:	Arkansas Home Equity Living Plan (AHELP)
PURPOSE OF PROGRAM:	To free up the equity in older person's homes so that needed cash is available for living expenses. In exchange for selling the remainder interest in their homes to ADFA, elderly participants retain a life estate, receive a monthly sum for life and ADFA pays real estate taxes, hazard insurance and necessary maintenance costs.
DATE BEGUN:	1985
AMOUNT OF FUNDING:	$5 million
SOURCE OF FUNDING:	Authority bond proceeds from past issues
ADDITIONAL INFO:	Eligible applicants must be at least 70 years old, and have an income of $15,000 or less for one person, or $22,500 for two. The house must have a minimum value of $20,000. Monthly payments and maintenance costs are established by a formula which calculates the present value of future sales proceeds.

Connecticut Housing Finance Authority

NAME OF PROGRAM:	Reverse Annuity Mortgage (RAM)
PURPOSE OF PROGRAM:	To enable senior citizens to convert their home's equity into a monthly tax-free cash payment for 10 years. Homeowners can borrow up to 80% of the value of the home and the loan typically will be repaid from the sale of the home. Loans are at 7% interest, with a monthly annuity of 0.4% of the home's appraised value. Maximum loan amount Is $80,000.
DATE BEGUN:	April 1985
AMOUNT OF FUNDING:	$20 million
SOURCE OF FUNDING:	Authority bond proceeds from past issues
ACTIVITY TO DATE:	Over 130 low-income elderly homeowners have benefited from this program.
ADDITIONAL INFO:	Eligible applicants must be 65 years or older, and have an annual income of 50% or less of the area median income.

Illinois Housing Development Authority

NAME OF PROGRAM:	Congregate Housing Finance Program
PURPOSE OF PROGRAM:	To finance congregate housing for the elderly in conjunction with FHA 221(d)(4) Retirement Service Center program.
DATE BEGUN:	1986
AMOUNT OF FUNDING:	$25 million
SOURCE OF FUNDING:	IDBs
ACTIVITY TO DATE:	Two projects, totaling 370 units, have been financed for a total loan amount of $25 million.

Kentucky Housing Corporation

NAME OF PROGRAM: Grants to the Elderly for Energy Repairs (GEER)
DATE BEGUN: 1984
AMOUNT OF FUNDING: $1 million was available through FY 1987
SOURCE OF FUNDING: Corporation reserves
ACTIVITY TO DATE: Over 600 elderly households have been assisted under the program.

Kentucky Housing Corporation

NAME OF PROGRAM: Senior Homeownership Program
PURPOSE OF PROGRAM: To provide lower interest rates on mortgage loans to homebuyers aged 62 and over. Interest rate depends on individual's ability to pay.
DATE BEGUN: October 1986
AMOUNT OF FUNDING: $1 million
SOURCE OF FUNDING: Kentucky Housing Trust Fund (funded through Corporation reserves)
ACTIVITY TO DATE: 6 loans with an average mortgage of $37,611 have been approved. Funds for an additional 5 loans have been set aside.
ADDITIONAL INFO: Average borrower monthly income is $650.00, which is primarily social security. Borrowers have limited savings and most are retired.

Maryland Community Development Administration

NAME OF PROGRAM: Elderly Rental Housing Program
PURPOSE OF PROGRAM: To provide financing for new construction and substantial rehabilitation of rental housing for elderly citizens with incomes between $4,000 and $10,000 per year.
DATE BEGUN: 1984
AMOUNT OF FUNDING: $1 million
SOURCE OF FUNDING: General obligation bonds
ACTIVITY TO DATE: 213 elderly units have been financed.
ADDITIONAL INFO: Developers must give a 10-year commitment to rent units to elderly tenants.

Oregon Housing Division

NAME OF PROGRAM:	Elderly and Disabled Housing Program
PURPOSE OF PROGRAM:	To develop and finance multifamily congregate housing for the elderly as an alternative to nursing homes. The program also finances residential care facilities for the frail elderly and group care homes for disabled persons.
DATE BEGUN:	1978
AMOUNT OF FUNDING:	Over $77 million
SOURCE OF FUNDING:	General obligation bonds
ACTIVITY TO DATE:	2,305 units for elderly and disabled households have been financed as of 12/31/86.

Rhode Island Housing and Mortgage Finance Corporation

NAME OF PROGRAM:	Elderly Home Equity Program
PURPOSE OF PROGRAM:	To provide reverse annuity mortgages to senior citizens who are homeowners and would otherwise be forced to sell their homes.
DATE BEGUN:	1986
AMOUNT OF FUNDING:	$5 million
SOURCE OF FUNDING:	A trust fund will be established to fund this on a permanent basis.
ACTIVITY TO DATE:	33 applications have been made, and 14 loans closed.
ADDITIONAL INFO:	Eligible applicants must be at least 68 years of age. Income limits for participation are $15,900 for one borrower, or $18,150 for co-borrowers. Maximum loan amount is $60,000. Interest rate on the loans is 7%, and borrowers may choose a 10-, 15- or 20-year mortgage term.

Appendix C
Reverse Mortgage Lenders List
(By State)

Prepared by the AARP Home Equity Information Center

This list identifies lenders who are presently offering or about to offer various types of reverse mortgages (RMs) as of December, 1994. As you will see, most lenders offer the FHA-insured Home Equity Conversion Mortgage (HECM). We will update this list periodically to reflect any changes in lender activity. In states where no lenders are active, it is not likely that lenders in adjacent states could make RMs across state lines, unless already noted on this list.

This list also includes information on the independent RM counseling agencies (ICA) who, in most cases, also serve as initial points for local fixed-term (FT) RM lenders in their areas. It is not practical to list all HUD-approved counseling agencies on this list as they number over 700. Contact the participating FHA/HECM lenders listed under your state directly for information on the geographic areas they serve and on counselors in your area. *See pages 166-68 for further information and definitions.* AARP does *not* endorse or support any individual reverse mortgage lender or product. This list is for informational purposes only.

	LOCATION	PHONE NUMBER	CONTACT	TYPE
ALABAMA				
Amerifirst Mortgage	Hempstead, NY	(800) 473-6476	HECM Sales Rep.	HECM
Home Mortgagee	Levittown, NY	(800) 669-8226	Sondra Geller	HECM
Homestead Mortgage	Columbus, GA	(706) 324-2274	John McEachern	HECM
Senior Income RM Corp.	Chicago	(800) 774-6266	Jeffrey Davis	HECM
United Savings Bank	Anniston	(205) 237-6668	Linda Harris	HECM
Reverse Mortgage Co.	Birmingham	(800) 588-8044	Douglas Cox	HECM

ALASKA

No RM Lenders at this time.

ARIZONA

Directors Mortgage	Ahwatukee	(800) 442-4966 x2201	Roger Reynolds	HECM
	Bullhead City	(602) 763-7000	Jerry Snider	HECM
	Flagstaff	(800) 442-4966 x2201	Roger Reynolds	HECM
	Glendale	(800) 442-4966 x2201	Roger Reynolds	HECM
	Kingman	(602) 763-7000	Jerry Snider	HECM
	Lake Havasu	(602) 763-7000	Jerry Snider	HECM
	Phoenix	(800) 442-4966 x2201	Roger Reynolds	HECM
	Riverside, CA	(800) 442-4966 x2201	Roger Reynolds	HECM
	Yuma	(602) 763-7000	Jerry Snider	HECM
Farwest Mortgage Inc.	Scottsdale	(619) 967-6951	Jim Keith	HECM
First Mortgage Corporation	Tempe	(800) 456-0569	Jim Laws	HECM
Household Senior Services	Phoenix (1/95)	(800) 414-3837	Dan Farnesi	EY(1/95)
Sun American Mortgage	Mesa	(602) 832-4343	Terry Turk	HECM
The Reverse Mortgage Co.	Portland, OR	(800) 334-9057	Sarah Howard	HECM
Reverse Mortgage Program	Tucson	(602) 623-0344 x376	Kay White	ICA
	Phoenix	(602) 997-1605	Mary Ellen Ondo	ICA
WestAmerica Mortgage Co.	Scottsdale	(800) 999-2649	Eric Moore	HECM

ARKANSAS

Amerifirst Mortgage	Hempstead, NY	(800) 473-6467	HECM Sales Rep.	HECM
Home Mortgagee	Levittown, NY	(800) 669-8226	Sondra Geller	HECM
Senior Income RM Corp.	Chicago, IL	(800) 774-6266	Grace Hartnedy	HECM
The Reverse Mortgage Co.	Little Rock	(800) 336-3135	Lyn Link (Mr.)	HECM
	Rogers	(800) 336-3135	Lyn Link (Mr.)	HECM

CALIFORNIA

ARCS Mortgage, Inc.	Bakersfield	(805) 395-0785	George Leckner	HECM
(*Corporate Office)	*Calabasas	(818) 880-2890	Harvey Parnell	HECM
	Covina	(818) 331-0991	Crystal Flynn	HECM
	Fresno	(209) 432-2727	Robert Zuercher	HECM
	Irvine	(714) 476-0367	Nancy Otjen	HECM
	Merced	(209) 384-8650	Janet Williams	HECM
	Modesto	(209) 575-4801	Janet Williams	HECM
	Paso Robles	(805) 238-5004	Fred Bond	HECM
	Pleasanton	(510) 847-2082	Michael Green	HECM
	Redding	(916) 223-2065	Lorraine Perales	HECM
	Sacramento	(916) 781-2727	Sean O'Hara	HECM
	Salinas	(408) 755-7940	Lauri Perkins	HECM
	San Diego	(619) 279-1701	Maureen Webster	HECM
	San Luis Obispo	(805) 543-2727	Fred Bond	HECM
	Santa Barbara	(805) 965-6699	William LaRocco	HECM

	Santa Maria	(805) 928-5727	William LaRocco	HECM
	Santa Rosa	(707) 546-4456	Tom Andrews	HECM
	Stockton	(209) 474-6161	Fred Womack	HECM
	Temecula	(909) 695-2727	Karen Davis	HECM
	Vallejo	(707) 557-2100	Michael Green	HECM
	Van Nuys	(818) 787-7723	John Lucas	HECM
Bank of Lodi	Lodi	(209) 367-2075	Christina Jay	HECM
CFE Mortgage	Pasadena	(818) 577-0233	Katherine Luna	HECM
	Pasadena	(800) 576-4233	Bonnie Robie	HECM
Directors Mortgage	Anaheim	(800) 442-4966 x2201	Roger Reynolds	HECM
	Arcadia	(800) 442-4966 x2201	Roger Reynolds	HECM
	Auburn	(800) 442-4966 x2201	Roger Reynolds	HECM
	Bakersfield	(800) 442-4966 x2201	Roger Reynolds	HECM
	Barstow	(619) 343-1420	Don Ketchem	HECM
	Big Bear	(800) 442-4966 x2201	Roger Reynolds	HECM
	Bonita	(619) 297-8880	Jay Tarvin	HECM
	Commerce	(800) 442-4966 x2201	Roger Reynolds	HECM
	Covina	(800) 442-4966 x2201	Roger Reynolds	HECM
	Escondido	(619) 297-8880	Jay Tarvin	HECM
	Fontana	(800) 442-4966 x2201	Roger Reynolds	HECM
	Fresno	(800) 442-4966 x2201	Roger Reynolds	HECM
	Hemet	(800) 442-4966 x2201	Roger Reynolds	HECM
	Indio	(619) 343-1420	Don Ketchem	HECM
	Lancaster	(800) 442-4966 x2201	Roger Reynolds	HECM
	Lompoc	(800) 442-4966 x1252	Bernie Murray	HECM
	Madera	(800) 442-4966 x2201	Roger Reynolds	HECM
	Mira Mesa	(619) 297-8880	Jay Tarvin	HECM
	Moreno Valley	(800) 442-4966 x2201	Roger Reynolds	HECM
	Mt. Shasta	(800) 442-4966 x2201	Roger Reynolds	HECM
	Newhall	(800) 442-4966 x2201	Roger Reynolds	HECM
	Oceanside	(619) 431-5330	Anne Carroll	HECM
	Palm Desert	(619) 343-1420	Don Ketchem	HECM
	Paradise	(800) 442-4966 x2201	Roger Reynolds	HECM
	Placerville	(800) 442-4966 x1248	Phil Bennett	HECM
	Point West	(800) 442-4966 x1249	Anita Bennett	HECM
	Rancho Cucamonga	(800) 442-4966 x2201	Roger Reynolds	HECM
	Redding	(800) 442-4966 x2201	Roger Reynolds	HECM
	Riverside	(800) 442-4966 x2201	Roger Reynolds	HECM
	Roseville	(800) 442-4966 x2201	Roger Reynolds	HECM
	Sacramento	(800) 442-4966 x1249	Anita Bennett	HECM
	San Bernardino	(800) 442-4966 x2201	Roger Reynolds	HECM
	San Diego	(619) 431-5330	Anne Carroll	HECM
	San Francisco	(800) 442-4966 x1248	Phil Bennett	HECM
	San Jose	(800) 442-4966 x2201	Roger Reynolds	HECM
	Santa Ana	(800) 442-4966 x2201	Roger Reynolds	HECM
	Santa Cruz	(800) 442-4966 x2201	Roger Reynolds	HECM
	Santa Maria	(800) 442-4966 x2201	Roger Reynolds	HECM
	Stockton	(800) 442-4966 x2201	Roger Reynolds	HECM
	Temecula	(800) 442-4966 x2201	Roger Reynolds	HECM
	Upland	(800) 442-4966 x2201	Roger Reynolds	HECM
	Van Nuys	(800) 442-4966 x2201	Roger Reynolds	HECM
	Ventura	(800) 442-4966 x2201	Roger Reynolds	HECM
	Victorville	(619) 343-1420	Don Ketchem	HECM

	Walnut Creek	(800) 442-4966 x1248	Phil Bennett	HECM
	Westlake Village	(800) 442-4966 x2201	Roger Reynolds	HECM
	Whittier	(800) 442-4966 x2201	Roger Reynolds	HECM
	Yreka	(800) 442-4966 x2201	Roger Reynolds	HECM
	Yucca Valley	(619) 343-1420	Don Ketchem	HECM
Farwest Mortgage Bankers	Laguna Hills	(714) 588-6784	Barbara Howard	HECM
	Oceanside	(619) 967-6951	Dean Jones	HECM
	Placentia	(714) 579-1177	Larry McNally	HECM
	Redondo Beach	(310) 316-8503	John Gregerson	HECM
	or	(800) 310-5568	John Gregerson	HECM
	Santa Maria	(805) 928-6711	Robert Frost	HECM
	Walnut	(909) 598-1662	John Hurley	HECM
First Priority Financial	Dublin	(510) 829-5620	Harry Molz	HECM
Household Senior Services	SF/LA/San Diego	(800) 414-3837	Dan Farnesi	EY(1/95)
Interstate Mortgage	Upland	(909) 982-4424	Don Jacobsen	HECM
Mical Mortgage	San Diego	(619) 627-1950	J.D. Willis	HECM
Northpoint Mortgage	Fresno	(209) 225-2255	Richard Ransom	HECM
Senior Income RM Corp.	Chicago, IL	(800) 774-6266	Shannon Tumpane	HECM
ShelterNet Inc.	San Mateo	(415) 525-2750	John Lenz	HECM
Skyvalley Financial	Vallejo	(800) 562-6390	Ellen Clouse	HECM
Unity/Reverse Mortgage Co.	Mission Viejo	(800) 334-9057	Karen Kasa	HECM
	Palo Alto	(800) 334-9057	Forest Scholpp	HECM
Village Realty & Home Loan	San Jose	(408) 274-3081	Philip Hawkinson	HECM
Senior Loan Center	Sacramento	(916) 971-9000	Lloyd Daniel	HECM
Transamerica HomeFirst HECM	San Francisco	(800) 538-5569	(Sales Rep.)	THF/
Freedom Home Equity Partners	Irvine	(800) 637-3336	(Sales Rep.)	FP
Life Services, Inc.	Glendale	(818) 547-0585	Bonnie Dingivan	FT
ECHO Housing	Oakland	(510) 271-7931	Eileen Cordova	ICA
HIP	San Mateo	(415) 348-6660	Judy Gaither	ICA
Independent Living Res. Ctr.	San Francisco	(415) 863-0581	Connie Munoz	ICA
Project Match	Santa Clara	(408) 287-7121	Juana Aranda (Friday Only)	ICA

COLORADO

Amerifirst Mortgage Corp.	Hempstead, NY	(800) 473-6467	HECM Sales Rep.	HECM
Directors Mortgage	Breckenridge	(800) 442-4966 x2201	Roger Reynolds	HECM
	Denver	(800) 442-4966 x2201	Roger Reynolds	HECM
	Durango	(800) 442-4966 x2201	Roger Reynolds	HECM
	Fort Collins	(800) 442-4966 x2201	Roger Reynolds	HECM
	Grand Junction	(800) 442-4966 x2201	Roger Reynolds	HECM
	Steamboat	(800) 442-4966 x2201	Roger Reynolds	HECM
	Telluride	(800) 442-4966 x2201	Roger Reynolds	HECM
	Vail	(800) 442-4966 x2201	Roger Reynolds	HECM
Home Mortgagee Corp.	Levittown, NY	(800) 669-8226	Sondra Geller	HECM
Unity/Mortgage Corp.	Boulder	(800) 358-8012	Jeffrey Moulton	HECM
	Denver/Thornton	(800) 358-8012	Ronnie Lawler	HECM
	Colorado Springs	(800) 358-8012	Fred Vice	HECM
	N. Colorado	(800) 358-8012	Eddie Jo Yost	HECM
Wendover Funding	Englewood	(800) 843-0480	Paulette Wisch	HECM

CONNECTICUT

Amerifirst Mortgage	Hempstead, NY	(800) 473-6467	HECM Sales Rep.	HECM
ARCS Mortgage	Hartford	(203) 659-8800	Todd Walters	HECM
Constitution Mtg. Bankers	Meriden	(203) 237-0007	Don Donnelly	HECM
CT Housing Finance Authority	Rocky Hill	(800) 443-9946	Linda Iglesias	SSL
Hartford Funding	Ronkonkoma, NY	(516) 588-9300	Regina Mangine	HECM
Home Mortgagee Corp.	Levittown, NY	(800) 669-8226	Sondra Geller	HECM
Peoples Savings Bank	New Britain	(203) 224-7771	Suzanne Marzi	HECM
Farmers & Mech. Bank	Middletown	(203) 346-9677	Dick Hetrick	FT
Peoples Bank	Hartford	(203) 328-7295	Cynthia Ziehl	FT
		or (800) 338-7366 (in CT)	Cynthia Ziehl	FT

DELAWARE

Amerifirst Mortgage	Hempstead, NY	(800) 473-6467	HECM Sales Rep.	HECM
Boulevard Mortgage	Trevose, PA	(215) 633-8080	Helene Tracy	HECM
Hart Mortgage	Marlton, NJ	(800) 666-4133	Delores Keaton	HECM
Home Mortgagee Corp.	Levittown, NY	(516) 796-6100	Sondra Geller	HECM
International Mortgage	Owings Mills, MD	(410) 581-7806	George Conover	HECM
		or (800) 581-7806	George Conover	HECM
Phoenix Mortgage	Ft. Washington, PA	(800) 427-0800	John F. Brady	HECM

DISTRICT OF COLUMBIA

Amerifirst Mortgage	Hempstead, NY	(800) 473-6467	HECM Sales Rep.	HECM
International Mortgage	Owings Mills, MD	(410) 581-7806	George Conover	HECM
		or (800) 581-7806	George Conover	HECM
Unity/Reverse Mortgage Co.	Rockville, MD	(800) 368-3254	Patty Wills	HECM

FLORIDA

Amerifirst Mortgage	Hempstead, NY	(800) 473-6467	HECM Sales Rep.	HECM
Bank of America Mortgage	Fort Myers	(813) 482-8686	Ed Kiedrowski	HECM
Brasota Mortgage	Bradenton	(813) 746-6119	William Morrison	HECM
Builders Finance, Ltd.	Plantation	(800) 538-1815	Don Moroney	HECM
Congress Funding Corporation	Clearwater	(813) 468-8791	Barbara Ross	HECM
Golden Age Mortgage	Boca Raton	(407) 392-9202	Kenneth Bassin	EY
Homeowners & Investors Svcs.	Lake Worth	(407) 533-6070	Herv Hugee	HECM
Household Senior Services	Ft. Myers/Naples	(800) 414-3837	Dan Farnesi	EY(1/9)
	Miami/Orlando	(800) 414-3837	Dan Farnesi	EY(1/9)
	Tampa/St. Pete.	(800) 414-3837	Dan Farnesi	EY(1/9)
		or (800) 435-2877	Ed Kiedrowski	HECM
	Ft. Lauderdale	(305) 772-3877	Elly Shea	HECM
Lincoln Financial	Seminole	(813) 399-0071	Ed Sullivan	HECM
Pinnacle Financial	Orlando	(407) 578-2000	Michael Noel	HECM
		or (800) 421-5626	Michael Noel	HECM

Pointe Federal Savings Bank	Boca Raton	(407) 395-3155	Darryl Hollis	HECM
Realco Mortgage Services	Jupiter	(407) 745-1769	Neil Petri	EY
Unity/Reverse Mortgage Co.	Jacksonville	(800) 249-4961	Jeanette Dykes	HECM
	Orlando	(800) 588-8044	Jay Marles	HECM
Value Financial Mortgage	Miami	(305) 444-8569	Daniel Bellina	EY

GEORGIA

Allatoona Federal Svgs. Bk.	Marietta	(404) 952-0606	George Phelps	HECM
Amerifirst Mortgage	Hempstead, NY	(800) 473-6476	HECM Sales Rep.	HECM
Home Mortgagee Corp.	Levittown, NY	(800) 669-8226	Sondra Geller	HECM
Homestead Mortgage	Columbus	(706) 324-2274	Don McEarchern	HECM
Sunshine Mortgage	Marietta	(404) 429-0255 x3601	Bill Weaver	HECM
	or	(800) 966-0255	Bill Weaver	HECM
Tucker Federal	Tucker	(404) 938-1222	Ron Edgin	HECM
Unity/Reverse Mortgage Co.	Atlanta	(800) 588-8044	Tracy Wise	HECM
	Savannah	(800) 588-8044	Nori Tilley	HECM

HAWAII

ARCS Mortgage	Kailua	(808) 263-6602	Brenda Reynolds	HECM
Directors Mortgage	Honolulu	(800) 442-4966 x2201	Roger Reynolds	HECM
First Hawaiian Mtg.	Honolulu	(808) 536-8899	Mary Jo Sato	HECM
	Kaiwa-Kona	(808) 329-7777	Judi Grandenz	HECM
	Kahului	(808) 871-7195	George Lindell	HECM
	Kamuela	(808) 885-7700	Peggy Cole	HECM
	Aiea	(808) 483-5511	Steve Higa	HECM
	Merced, CA	(209) 725-8590	Dianna Vargas	HECM
	Roseville, CA	(916) 786-6400	Bob Gadberrry	HECM
U.S. Financial Mtg. Corp.	Tahoe City, CA	(916) 581-5626	Jeff Uldricks	HECM
	Kahului	(808) 871-7195	Shirley Christiansen	HECM

IDAHO

Amerifirst Mortgage	Hempstead, NY	(800) 473-6467	HECM Sales Rep.	HECM
Directors Mortgage	Coeur d'Alene	(800) 442-4966 x2201	Roger Reynolds	HECM
	Twin Falls	(800) 442-4966 x2201	Roger Reynolds	HECM
Home Mortgagee Corp.	Levittown, NY	(800) 669-8226	Sondra Geller	HECM
Investors West Mortgage	Boise	(208) 345-8153	Jim Spicka	HECM
	or	(800) 281-3338 (ID *only*)	Jim Spicka	HECM
The Reverse Mortgage Co.	Portland, OR	(800) 334-9057	Sarah Howard	HECM

ILLINOIS

Amerifirst Mortgage	Hempstead, NY	(800) 473-6467	HECM Sales Rep.	HECM
Berkshire Mortgage Corp.	Hinsdale	(708) 323-3400	Sharon Golz	EY
Dependable Mortgage	Calumet City	(708) 862-5969	Phillip Berenc	HECM
Directors Mortgage	Chicago	(800) 442-4966 x2201	Roger Reynolds	HECM
	Glen Ellyn	(800) 442-4966 x2201	Roger Reynolds	HECM
	Schaumburg	(800) 442-4966 x2201	Roger Reynolds	HECM
First Suburban Mortgage	Inverness	(708) 934-1111	Frank J. Moncey	HECM/EY
		or (800) 600-8333	Martin Welfeld	HECM/EY
Household Senior Services	Rolling Meadows	(708) 734-7941	Greg Walsh	EY
NBD Bank	Park Ridge	(708) 518-7100	Eric Johnson	HECM
Senior Income RM Corp.	Chicago	(800) 774-6266	Mary Ressetar	HECM/EY
Unity/Reverse Mortgage Co.	Madison, WI	(800) 800-7740	Michael B. Sands	HECM
WestAmerica Mortgage Co.	Oakbrook Terrace	(800) 999-2649	Eric Moore	HECM

INDIANA

Dependable Mortgage Co.	Calumet City, IL	(708) 862-5969	Phillip Berenc	HECM
Home Mortgagee	Levittown, NY	(800) 669-8226	Sondra Geller	HECM
Homeowners Mortgage	Indianapolis	(317) 580-2250	Don Austill	HECM
Senior Income RM Corp.	Chicago, IL	(800) 774-6266	Karen Sanford	HECM
Unity/Reverse Mortgage Co.	Indianapolis	(800) 860-6983	Rob Bickel	HECM
WestAmerica Mortgage Co.	Oakbrook Terr., IL	(800) 999-2649	Eric Moore	HECM

IOWA

Allied Group Mtg. Co.	W. Des Moines	(515) 224-7100	Joanne Konz	HECM
Commercial Federal	Omaha	(402) 554-9200	Don Dugger	HECM
Senior Income RM Corp.	Chicago, IL	(800) 774-6266	Robert Bottke	HECM
WestAmerica Mortgage Co.	Davenport	(800) 999-2649	Eric Moore	HECM

KANSAS

Amerifirst Mortgage	Hempstead, NY	(800) 473-6467	HECM Sales Rep.	HECM
Directors Mortgage	Kansas City	(913) 338-5060	Jim Scaletty	HECM
	Topeka	(913) 338-5060	Jim Scaletty	HECM
Home Mortgagee Corp.	Levittown, NY	(516) 796-6100	Sondra Geller	HECM
James B. Nutter & Co.	Kansas City	(816) 531-2345	Chuck Hendricks	HECM
Senior Income RM Corp.	Chicago, IL	(800) 774-6266	Dorothy Baum	HECM
The Reverse Mortgage Co.	Kansas City	(800) 336-3135	Lyn Link (Mr.)	HECM
	Wichita	(800) 336-3135	Lyn Link (Mr.)	HECM

KENTUCKY

Amerifirst Mortgage	Hempstead, NY	(800) 473-6467	HECM Sales Rep.	HECM
Home Mortgagee	Levittown, NY	(800) 669-8226	Sondra Geller	HECM
Senior Income RM Corp.	Chicago, IL	(800) 774-6255	Cathy Boone	HECM
Tri-County Mortgage	Corbin	(606) 523-1076	Joan Barton	HECM
Unity/Reverse Mortgage Co.	Cleveland, OH	(800) 360-6983	Ken Sawan	HECM

LOUISIANA

Amerifirst Mortgage	Hempstead, NY	(800) 473-6467	HECM Sales Rep.	HECM
Home Mortgagee	Metairie	(504) 830-4747	Alison Borges	HECM
Mortgage Co-op Inc.	Metairie	(504) 455-4000	Louis Wolfort	HECM
The Reverse Mtg. Co.	Lake Charles	(800) 336-3135	Lyn Link (Mr.)	HECM
	New Orleans	(800) 336-3135	Lyn Link (Mr.)	HECM
	Shreveport	(800) 336-3135	Lyn Link (Mr.)	HECM

MAINE

Maine State Housing Auth.	Augusta	(207) 623-2981	Debbie King	HECM
Unity/Reverse Mortgage Co.	Bedford, NH	(800) 832-5251	Joseph Ferris	HECM
Gardner Savings Institution	Gardner	(207) 882-7571	Jeannine Clark	FT

MARYLAND

Amerifirst Mortgage	Hempstead, NY	(800) 473-6467	HECM Sales Rep.	HECM
Bank United Mortgage	Virginia Beach, VA	(800) 282-4326	Martin Principe	HECM
Carroll County Bank	Westminster	(410) 857-3470	Diane Dabney	HECM
HEC of Maryland	Annapolis	(410) 269-4322	Bill Hamilton	HECM
		or (800) 310-4322 (in MD)	Bill Hamilton	HECM
Home Mortgagee Corp.	Levittown, NY	(516) 796-6100	Sondra Geller	HECM
	Rockville	(800) 368-3254	Patty Wills	HECM/EY
Household Bank	Baltimore	(410) 484-1770	Ilene Bard	EY
	Baltimore	(410) 282-5000	Pat Walczak	EY
	Columbia	(410) 730-9111	Waqlly Daley	EY
International Mortgage	Baltimore	(800) 581-7806	George Conover	HECM
	Cumberland	(301) 777-1400	Barbara Wiseman	HECM
	Owings Mills	(410) 581-7806	George Conover	HECM
Unity/Reverse Mortgage Co.	Columbia	(800) 368-3254	Emmett Coyne	HECM/EY

MASSACHUSETTS

Amerifirst Mortgage	Hempstead, NY	(800) 473-6467	HECM Sales Rep.	HECM
H.O.M.E.	Boston	(617) 451-0680	Cornelia Patten	ICA

MICHIGAN

Bay Creek Mortgage	Gresham, OR	(503) 492-3900	Greg Cox	HECM
	Grand Rapids	(800) 968-5151	Ken Kuszpit	HECM
Home Mortgagee Corp.	Levittown, NY	(516) 796-6100	Sondra Geller	HECM/EY
Household Senior Services	Detroit	(800) 414-3837	Dan Farnesi	EY (1/95)
North Bank	Rose City	(517) 685-3519	Scott Pauly	HECM
Senior Income RM Corp.	Chicago, IL	(800) 774-6266	Eileen Stockman	HECM
Unity/Reverse Mortgage Co.	Detroit	(800) 433-8485	Lisa Neuman	HECM/EY

MINNESOTA

Amerifirst Mortgage	Hempstead, NY	(800) 473-6467	HECM Sales Rep.	HECM
Directors Mortgage	Riverside, CA	(800) 442-4966 x2201	Roger Reynolds	HECM
Heigl Mortgage	Bloomington	(612) 831-6644	Brad Anderson	HECM
Home Mortgagee Corp.	Levittown, NY	(800) 669-8226	Sondra Geller	HECM
Richfield Bank and Trust	Richfield	(612) 798-3339	Joan Berglund	HECM

MISSISSIPPI

Amerifirst Mortgage Corp.	Hempstead, NY	(800) 473-6467	HECM Sales Rep.	HECM
Unity/Reverse Mortgage Co.	Jackson	(800) 533-7771	Nancy Canterbury	HECM

MISSOURI

Amerifirst Mortgage Corp.	Hempstead, NY	(800) 473-6467	HECM Sales Rep.	HECM
Directors Mortgage	Gladstone	(913) 338-5060	Jim Scaletty	HECM
	Independence	(913) 338-5060	Jim Scaletty	HECM
	Kansas City	(913) 338-5060	Jim Scaletty	HECM
	Springfield	(913) 338-5060	Jim Scaletty	HECM
	St. Louis	(800) 442-4966 x2201	Roger Reynolds	HECM
Home Mortgagee Corp.	Levittown, NY	(800) 669-8226	Sondra Geller	HECM
James B. Nutter & Company	Kansas City	(816) 531-2345	Chuck Hendricks	HECM
Senior Income RM Corp.	Chicago, IL	(800) 774-6266	Cindy Donohue	HECM
The Reverse Mortgage Co.	Columbia	(800) 336-3135	Lyn Link (Mr.)	HECM
	Joplin	(800) 336-3135	Lyn Link (Mr.)	HECM
	Kansas City	(800) 336-3135	Lyn Link (Mr.)	HECM
	Springfield	(800) 336-3135	Lyn Link (Mr.)	HECM
	St. Louis	(800) 336-3135	Lyn Link (Mr.)	HECM

MONTANA

Amerifirst Mortgage Corp.	Hempstead, NY	(800) 473-6467	HECM Sales Rep.	HECM
Board of Housing	Helena	(406) 444-3040	Richard Kain	SSL
Intermountain Mortgage	Billings	(406) 252-2600	Suzanne Redinger	HECM
The Reverse Mortgage Co.	Portland, OR	(800) 334-9057	Sarah Howard	HECM

NEBRASKA

Amerifirst Mortgage Corp.	Hempstead, NY	(800) 473-6467	HECM Sales Rep.	HECM
Commercial Federal	Omaha	(402) 554-9200	Don Dugger	HECM
Unity/Reverse Mortgage Co.	Boulder, CO	(800) 358-8012	Jeffrey Moulton	HECM

NEVADA

ARCS Mortgage	Las Vegas	(702) 877-0556	Daniel Callihan	HECM
Directors Mortgage	Carson City	(800) 442-4966 x2201	Roger Reynolds	HECM
	Elko	(800) 442-4966 x2201	Roger Reynolds	HECM
	Incline Village	(800) 442-4966 x2201	Roger Reynolds	HECM
	Las Vegas	(702) 454-2870	Sandy Rhody	HECM
	Reno	(800) 442-4966 x2201	Roger Reynolds	HECM
	Riverside, CA	(800) 442-4966 x2201	Roger Reynolds	HECM
The Reverse Mortgage Co.	Portland, OR	(800) 334-9057	Sarah Howard	HECM
WestAmerica Mortgage	Las Vegas	(702) 796-7990	Lucy Jelcz	HECM

NEW HAMPSHIRE

CFX Bank	Keene	(603) 352-2502	William Dennison	HECM
Chittenden Bank	Burlington, VT	(802) 660-2123	Jenny Buchanon	HECM
Directors Mortgage	Bedford	(800) 442-4966 x2201	Roger Reynolds	HECM
First Deposit Natl. Bank	Tilton	(603) 286-4348 x11	Denise Hubbard	HECM
Home Mortgagee Corp.	Levittown, NY	(800) 669-8226	Sondra Geller	HECM
Unity/Reverse Mortgage Co.	Bedford	(800) 832-5251	Patti Clark	HECM/EY
N.H. Housing Fin. Agency	Manchester	(800) 640-7239	Brenda Mahoney	SSL

NEW JERSEY

Amerifirst Mortgage	Hempstead, NY	(800) 473-6467	HECM Sales Rep.	HECM
ARCS Mortgage	Totowa	(201) 812-5550	Bill Calderara	HECM
		or (201) 812-5500	Edward LePore	HECM
Boulevard Mortgage	Trevose, PA	(215) 633-8080	Helene Tracy	HECM
Foremost Mortgage	Shrewsbury	(908) 842-8600	Stephen Dexter	HECM
		or (800) 414-6678	Stephen Dexter	HECM
Hart Mortgage	Wanague	(201) 492-2328	Jim Vance	HECM
	Marlton	(800) 666-4133	Delores Keaton	HECM

Household Senior Services	Chicago, IL	(800) 414-3837	Dan Farnesi	EY(1/95)
Interchange State Bank	Saddlebrook	(201) 845-5600	Len Ricci	HECM
Phoenix Mortgage	Ft. Washington, PA	(800) 427-0800	John F. Brady	HECM
	Willow Grove, PA	(215) 659-0800	Cindy Merrifield	HECM
Pioneer Mortgage	Haddon Hgts.	(609) 546-1700	Peter Malkasian	HECM
	Ft. Washington, PA	(800) 427-0800	John F. Brady	HECM
Transamerica HomeFirst THF	San Francisco, CA	(800) 538-5569	(Sales Rep.)	HECM/
Boiling Springs S&L	Rutherford	(201) 939-5000	Karl Becker	FT

NEW MEXICO

Amerifirst Mortgage	Hempstead, NY	(800) 473-6467	HECM Sales Rep.	HECM
Directors Mortgage	Riverside, CA	(800) 442-4966 x2201	Roger Reynolds	HECM
Home Mortgagee Corp.	Levittown, NY	(800) 669-8226	Sondra Geller	HECM

NEW YORK

Amerifirst Mortgage	Buffalo	(716) 852-3348	HECM Sales Rep.	HECM
	Hempstead	(800) 473-6467	HECM Sales Rep.	HECM
	Newburgh	(914) 562-1300	HECM Sales Rep.	HECM
	White Plains	(914) 328-7800	HECM Sales Rep.	HECM
	Schenectady	(518) 372-9501	HECM Sales Rep.	HECM
ARCS/Bank of N.Y. Mtg.	Newburgh	(914) 566-0100	Joanne Albert	HECM
	So. Westchester	(914) 631-5000	Larry Michaelessi	HECM
	Tarrytown	(914) 631-5000 x12	Mario Martirano	HECM
Country Bank	Carmel	(914) 225-2265	Thomas Berte	HECM
Hartford Funding	Ronkonkoma	(516) 988-9300	Regina Mangine	HECM
Home Mortgagee Corp.	Levittown	(516) 796-6100	Sondra Geller	HECM
	Flushing/Queens	(718) 997-7000	Sondra Geller	HECM
	Upstate	(800) 669-8226	Sondra Geller	HECM
	Westchester	(914) 948-4111	Sondra Geller	HECM
Household Senior Services	Chicago, IL	(800) 414-3837	Dan Farnesi	EY(1/95)
Onondaga Savings Bank	Syracuse	(315) 424-4011	Martha VanDuesen	HECM
Rockwell Equities	Jericho	(516) 334-7900	Al Geldmacher	HECM
Saxon National Mortgage Bank	Albany	(800) 660-1853	John Kane	HECM
	Hauppauge	(516) 231-0500 x662	Al Mandarino	HECM
	Staten Island	(718) 494-6698	Steve Polsky	HECM
Senior Income RM Corp.	Chicago, IL	(800) 774-6266	Mary Conaton	HECM
Transamerica HomeFirst THF	San Francisco, CA	(800) 538-5569	Sales Rep.	HECM/
Counseling for HEC	Hempstead	(516) 485-5600	Carol Griefer	ICA
Westchester Res. Hsg.	White Plains	(914) 428-0953	Doris Schear	ICA

NORTH CAROLINA

Centura Bank	Rocky Mount	(704) 396-2106	Teresa Tilley	HECM
		or (800) 879-5864	Teresa Tilley	HECM

Bank United Mortgage	Virginia Beach, VA	(800) 282-4326	Martin Principe	HECM
Financial First Fed. Sv. Bank	Burlington	(919) 227-8861	Mona Gunn	HECM
First Federal Savings	Charlotte	(704) 335-4400	Anelson Watkins	HECM
Home Mortgagee Corp.	Levittown, NY	(516) 796-6100	Sondra Geller	HECM
Unity/Reverse Mortgage Co.	Raleigh	(800) 588-8044	Brenda Phillips	HECM
Wendover Funding	Greensboro	(800) 283-4326 x2331	Pat Reed	HECM

NORTH DAKOTA

Directors Mortgage	Bismark	(800) 442-4966 x2201	Roger Reynolds	HECM
	Minot	(800) 442-4966 x2201	Roger Reynolds	HECM
	Riverside, CA	(800) 442-4966 x2201	Roger Reynolds	HECM

OHIO

Amerifirst Mortgage	Hempstead, NY	(800) 473-6467	HECM Sales Rep.	HECM
Excel Mortgage	Cleveland	(800) 573-8091	Chuck Pappadakes	HECM
Home Mortgagee Corp.	Levittown, NY	(800) 669-8226	Sondra Geller	HECM
Household Senior Services	Columbus	(800) 414-3837	Dan Farnesi	EY (1/95)
Senior Income RM Corp.	Chicago, IL	(800) 774-6266	Nancy Hunkler	HECM
Unity/Reverse Mortgage Co.	Canton	(800) 860-6983	Tammy Lawton	HECM
	Cleveland	(800) 860-6983	Ken Sawan	HECM/EY
	Cincinnati	(800) 860-6983	David Levy	HECM/EY
	Columbus	(800) 860-6983	Michael Kennedy	HECM/EY
	Southeast	(800) 860-6983	Richard Valentin	HECM/EY
	Toledo	(800) 860-6983	Andy Mungons	HECM/EY

OKLAHOMA

Amerifirst Mortgage Corp.	Hempstead, NY	(800) 473-6467	HECM Sales Rep.	HECM
Senior Income RM Corp.	Chicago, IL	(800) 774-6266	Betty McRae	HECM
The Reverse Mortgage Co.	Norman/Tulsa/ Oklahoma City	(800) 336-3135	Lyn Link (Mr.)	HECM

OREGON

Amerifirst Mortgage Corp.	Hempstead, NY	(800) 473-6467	HECM Sales Rep.	HECM
ARCS Mortgage	Grants Pass	(503) 471-2727	Mary Linton	HECM
	Medford	(503) 770-2727	Mary Linton	HECM
	Roseburg	(503) 673-0239	Mary Linton	HECM
	Bend	(503) 389-3323	Sandy Weich	HECM
Directors Mortgage	Klamath Falls	(800) 442-4966 x2201	Roger Reynolds	HECM
	Lake Oswego	(503) 526-1331	Lynn Wertzler	HECM
	La Pine	(800) 442-4966 x2201	Roger Reynolds	HECM
	Medford	(800) 442-4966 x2201	Roger Reynolds	HECM
	Portland	(503) 526-1331	Lynn Wertzler	HECM

	Riverside, CA	(800) 442-4966 x2201	Roger Reynolds	HECM
	Roseburg	(503) 526-1331	Lynn Wertzler	HECM
	Salem	(503) 526-1331	Lynn Wertzler	HECM
Home Mortgagee Corp.	Levittown, NY	(800) 669-8226	Sondra Geller	HECM
Investors West Mortgage	Boise, ID	(208) 345-8153	Jim Spicka	HECM
Unity/Reverse Mortgage Co.	Gresham	(800) 334-9057	Ron Richardson	HECM
	Portland	(800) 334-9057	Sarah Howard	HECM

PENNSYLVANIA

Affinity National Mortgage	Malvern	(215) 647-2056	Buck Jones	HECM
Amerifirst Mortgage	Hempstead, NY	(800) 473-6467	HECM Sales Rep.	HECM
Bank United Mortgage	Virginia Beach, VA	(800) 282-4326	Martin Principe	HECM
Boulevard Mortgage	Trevose	(800) 767-5664	Helene Tracy	HECM
Directors Mortgage	York	(800) 442-4966 x2201	Roger Reynolds	HECM
Hart Mortgage Corporation	Ft. Washington	(215) 628-3131	Delores Keaton	HECM
Home Mortgagee Corp.	Levittown, NY	(516) 796-6100	Sondra Geller	HECM
Household Senior Services	Philadelphia	(800) 414-3837	Dan Farnesi	EY (1/95)
International Mortgage	Cumberland, MD	(301) 777-1400	Barbara Wiseman	HECM
		or (800) 581-7806	Barbara Wiseman	HECM
Penn. Housing Finance Agency	Harrisburg	(800) 635-4747	Kimberly Green-Jones	HECM
Phoenix Mortgage	Ft. Washington	(800) 427-0800	John Brady	HECM
Pioneer Mortgage	Haddon Hts., NJ	(609) 546-1700	Peter Malkasian	HECM
		or (800) 222-0057 (in PA)	Peter Malkasian	HECM
Transamerica HomeFirst	San Francisco, CA	(800) 538-5569	(Sales Rep.)	HECM/
THF				
Unity/Reverse Mortgage Co.	Pittsburgh	(800) 487-0088	Gene Burke	HECM
	Philadelphia	(215) 674-1125	Rick Roode	HECM
		or (800) 487-0088	Rick Roode	HECM
WestAmerica Mortgage Co.	Aston Township	(800) 999-2649	Eric Moore	HECM

PUERTO RICO

Banco Popular	San Juan	(809) 765-9800	Pablo Montanez	HECM

RHODE ISLAND

Rhode Island Housing	Providence	(401) 751-5566 x257	Frank Soares	HECM

SOUTH CAROLINA

Amerifirst Mortgage Corp.	Hempstead, NY	(800) 473-6467	HECM Sales Rep.	HECM
American Federal Bank	Greenville	(803) 255-7434	Sharon King	HECM
		or (800) 726-6837	Sharon King	HECM
Home Mortgagee Corp.	Levittown, NY	(800) 669-8226	Sondra Geller	HECM
First Citizens Mtg. Corp.	Columbia	(803) 733-2778	Patti Adolphson	HECM

First Federal of Spartanburg	Spartanburg	(803) 582-2391	Brenda Mathis	HECM
The Reverse Mortgage Co.	Atlanta, GA	(800) 588-8044	Brenda Philips	HECM

SOUTH DAKOTA

No RM Lenders at this time.

TENNESSEE

Amerifirst Mortgage Corp.	Hempstead, NY	(800) 473-6467	HECM Sales Rep.	HECM
Bank United Mortgage	VA Beach, VA	(800) 282-4326	Joan Baliles	HECM
Home Mortgagee Corp.	Levittown, NY	(516) 796-6100	Sondra Geller	HECM
Mortgage South of TN	Chattanooga	(615) 624-3878	Cathy Richmond	HECM
Senior Income RM Corp.	Chicago, IL	(800) 774-6266	Joyce Baker	HECM
The Reverse Mortgage Co.	Knoxville/Chat.	(800) 588-8044	Pat Callahan	HECM

TEXAS

No RM lenders at this time. Texas has a Constitutional prohibition against almost all home equity loans, including RMs. For updates and current information, call Tim Simmons at AARP's Area Office in Dallas: 214/265-4060.

UTAH

Amerifirst Mortgage	Hempstead, NY	(800) 473-6467	HECM Sales Rep.	HECM
Affiliated Mortgage	Midvale	(801) 255-1118	Zed Braden	HECM
AIM Mortgage, Inc.	Salt Lake City	(801) 969-5000	Sonja Jeffs	HECM
		or (800) 505-5600	Sonja Jeffs	HECM
Directors Mortgage	Layton	(800) 442-4966 x2201	Roger Reynolds	HECM
	Midvale	(800) 442-4966 x2201	Roger Reynolds	HECM
	Provo	(800) 442-4966 x2201	Roger Reynolds	HECM
	St. George	(800) 442-4966 x2201	Roger Reynolds	HECM
	Riverside, CA	(800) 442-4966 x2201	Roger Reynolds	HECM
	Salt Lake City	(800) 442-4966 x2201	Roger Reynolds	HECM
		or (800) 442-4966	Roger Reynolds	HECM
	West Jordan	(800) 442-4966	Roger Reynolds	HECM
MultiServe Mortgage	Salt Lake City	(801) 222-3232	Larry Miller	HECM
	Orem	(801) 222-9393	Larry Miller	HECM

VERMONT

Amerifirst Mortgage	Hempstead, NY	(800) 473-6467	HECM Sales Rep.	HECM
Chittenden Bank	Burlington	(802) 660-2123	Jenny Buchanon	HECM
Unity/Reverse Mortgage Co.	Bedford, NH	(800) 832-5251	Patti Clark	HECM

VIRGINIA

Ameribanc Savings	Annandale	(703) 658-5500	Bonnie Gaitley	HECM
Bank United Mortgage	Virginia Beach	(800) 282-4326	Martin Principe	HECM
Crestar Mortgage Corp.	Virginia Beach	(800) 431-4876	Russell S. Heath	HECM
Directors Mortgage	Hampton	(800) 442-4966 x2201	Roger Reynolds	HECM
	Norfolk	(800) 442-4966 x2201	Roger Reynolds	HECM
	Richmond	(800) 442-4966 x2201	Roger Reynolds	HECM
	Virginia Beach	(800) 442-4966 x2201	Roger Reynolds	HECM
Dupont Fibers Fed. Cred. Un.	*Richmond	(804) 743-3590	Donna Etter	HECM
First VA Bank Colonial	Richmond	(804) 697-1652	Jeff Harris	HECM
First VA Bank of Tidewater	Norfolk	(804) 628-6636	Judy Ayers	HECM
Greater Atlantic Savings Bank	Herndon	(703) 318-8300	Robert Daniels	HECM
Home Mortgage Center	Alexandria	(703) 671-1414	Tom Ruppert	HECM
Home Mortgagee Corp.	Levittown, NY	(800) 669-8226	Sondra Geller	HECM
Household Bank	Alexandria	(703) 671-9335	Yung Ju West	EY
	Herndon	(703) 437-8001	Dana Vosburgh	EY
	Springfield	(703) 971-0110	Vicki Schofield	EY
International Mortgage	Owings Mills, MD	(410) 581-7806	George Conover	HECM
	Roanoke	(703) 981-1011	J.M. Anderson	HECM
Mortgage Capital Investors	Springfield	(703) 941-0711	Peter Ford	HECM
Unity/Reverse Mortgage Co.	McLean	(800) 368-3254	Gloria Cohan	HECM/EY
	Richmond	(800) 368-3254	Thelma Barbour	HECM/EY
Virginia Housing Dev. Auth.	Richmond	(804) 782-1986	Toni Ostrowski	HECM
	Abingdon	(703) 676-3668	Michael A. Locking	HECM
	Richlands	(703) 676-3668	George Godbey	HECM
	Urbanna	(804) 758-4025	Bruce DeSimone	HECM

*For credit union members only

WASHINGTON

ARCS Mortgage	Bellevue	(206) 462-7055	Ken Kiernan	HECM
	Lynnwood	(206) 744-2727	Jim Church	HECM
		or (800) 428-2727		
Directors Mortgage	Bellevue	(800) 310-4716	Jerry Capretta	HECM
	Eastgate	(206) 310-4716	Jerry Capretta	HECM
	Federal Way	(800) 329-6400	Jerry Capretta	HECM
	Kent	(206) 310-4716	Jerry Capretta	HECM
	Longview	(800) 442-4966 x1250	Roger Reynolds	HECM
	Lynnwood	(206) 778-3402	Jerry Capretta	HECM
	Northgate	(206) 310-4716	Jerry Capretta	HECM
	Richland	(800) 442-4966 x2201	Roger Reynolds	HECM
	Seattle	(206) 310-4716	Jerry Capretta	HECM
	Spokane	(800) 442-4966 x2201	Roger Reynolds	HECM
	Tacoma	(800) 329-6400	Jerry Capretta	HECM
	Vancouver	(503) 526-1331	Lynn Wertzler	HECM
Home Mortgagee Corp.	Levittown, NY	(800) 669-8226	Sondra Geller	HECM
Investors Mortgage	Boise, ID	(208) 345-8153	James Spicka	HECM
Senior Income RM Corp.	Chicago, IL	(800) 774-6266	Barbara Herring	HECM
Unity/Reverse Mortgage Co.	Portland, OR	(800) 334-9057	Sarah Howard	HECM
	Gig Harbor	(800) 334-9057	Bill Joyce	HECM
Western States Mortgage Corp.	Bellevue	(800) 828-2814	Christy Diemond	HECM

WEST VIRGINIA

Bank United Mortgage	Virginia Beach, VA	(800) 282-4326	Martin Principe	HECM
Home Mortgagee Corp.	Levittown, NY	(800) 669-8226	Sondra Geller	HECM
International Mortgage	Cumberland, MD	(301) 777-1400	Barbara Wiseman	HECM
	Owings Mills, MD	(800) 581-7806	George Conover	HECM
Senior Income RM Corp.	Chicago, IL	(800) 774-6266	Carolyn Benedict	HECM
Unity/Reverse Mortgage Co.	Charleston	(304) 343-6796	John Clancy	HECM
		or (800) 368-3254	John Clancy	HECM

WISCONSIN

Directors Mortgage	Wauwatosa	(800) 442-4966 x2201	Roger Reynolds	HECM
First Financial Bank	Milwaukee	(414) 547-9100	Kathy Knoebel	HECM
	Milwaukee	(414) 778-1610	Sharon Jaschob	HECM
Heigl Mortgage	Edina, MN	(612) 947-4010	Brad Anderson	HECM
Home Mortgagee Corp.	Levittown, NY	(516) 796-6100	Sondra Geller	HECM
IDL Bank of America	Madison	(608) 276-4646	Brenda Hollman	HECM
Senior Income RM Corp.	Chicago, IL	(800) 774-6266	Robin O'Keefe	HECM
Unity/Reverse Mortgage Co.	Madison	(608) 222-7740	Michael Sands	HECM
		or (800) 880-7740	Michael Sands	HECM
	Milwaukee	(414) 282-4813	Peter Pazucha	HECM/EY
WestAmerica Mortgage Co.	Oakbrook Terr., IL	(800) 999-2649	Eric Moore	HECM

WYOMING

Amerifirst Mortgage	Hempstead, NY	(800) 473-6467	HECM Sales Rep.	HECM
Home Mortgagee Corp.	Levittown, NY	(800) 669-8226	Sondra Geller	HECM
Unity/Reverse Mortgage Co.	Boulder, CO	(800) 358-8012	Jeffrey Moulton	HECM

PROGRAM AND SERVICE SUMMARIES

FHA-INSURED RM LENDER (HECM): Housing legislation passed by Congress in 1987 and amended in 1989 authorized 25,000 federally-insured reverse mortgages (RMs) under an expanded RM insurance program sponsored by the Federal Housing Administration (FHA) of the U.S. Department of Housing and Urban Development (HUD). The program is formally known as the Home Equity Conversion Mortgage (HECM) insurance demonstration. Earlier reservation and lottery limits established in 1987 have been lifted; any of the 10,000 HUD-approved mortgagees (lenders) can make these loans. The demonstration period has been extended to September, 1995. Proposals to extend the program or make it permanent are expected to be considered by the Congress during 1995. Almost 10,000 of these loans have been closed to date (12/94).

This list includes only FHA lenders who have already closed a HECM loan *AND* who intend to continue doing so—to the best of our knowledge. You can identify other FHA-approved lenders to encourage their participation by consulting the yellow pages under "Mortgages." Many lenders do not list their FHA-approval in their advertisements; contact lenders by telephone to see if they are 1) FHA-approved and 2) interested in offering these loans. If so, approved lenders should contact the nearest HUD Field Office, requesting Handbook 4235.1 REV-1 for details. New lenders who wish to become HUD-approved to offer these loans must call the Lender Approval and Recertification Division at HUD in Washington, D.C. (202/708-3976).

All eligible borrowers must be at least 62 years old. Only single family one-unit owner-occupied dwellings are eligible. Condominiums must be FHA-approved to be eligible. Mobile homes (not permanently affixed to a foundation), cooperatives and multiple unit dwellings are ineligible. Borrowers may receive cash advance monthly (for a fixed number of months or for as long as one borrower continues to live in the home), as a line-of-credit, or in a combination of monthly and line-of-credit basis. No repayment is required until the last surviving borrower dies, sells or moves permanently from the home. There are no maximum income limits for program participation (except in programs operated by housing finance agencies in Virginia and Rhode Island).

The amount of cash that homeowners can borrow is a percentage based on the lesser of their home value or an area limit [also known as the 203(b)(2) limit]. This limit is set by FHA and ranges in the Continental U.S. from $77,197 to $152,362. The percentage of this limit that any borrower can receive, given a 9.0% expected interest rate which is typical today, ranges from 30% of the 203(b) limit for a 62 year old to 80% of this limit for a 95 year old.

The HECM program also requires that homeowners receive counseling from a *HUD-approved counseling agency* prior to applying for a HECM from a participating lender. AARP has trained over 700 of these agencies over the past five years to provide this counseling. We are not able to print their names and addresses in our summary due to the large number of agencies; participating lenders will make referrals to the counseling agencies with trained staff or volunteers in their service areas.

FIXED TERM RM LENDER (FT): Some lending institutions offer reverse mortgages (RMs) that provide monthly payments for a fixed term, generally from three to ten years, as selected by the borrower. These loans are *not insured.* Repayment *is* required at the end of the loan term. Minimum ages for eligible borrowers generally range from 65 to 70.

SELF-INSURED REVERSE MORTGAGE LENDERS: Three private lenders offer proprietary reverse mortgages that do not include insurance from the federal government. Contact each lender directly for specific program details.

1. *THF—Transamerica HomeFirst,* headquartered in California, offers monthly advances for life or a line of credit.
2. *FP*—Freedom Home Equity Partners offers the *Freedom Plan* in California that provides a lump sum or monthly income for life.
3. *EY*—Household Senior Services offers *Ever Yours,* a credit line that does not have to be repaid as long as at least one borrower remains in the home. In some cases, multiple unit owner-occupied properties may be eligible.

INDEPENDENT COUNSELING AGENCY (ICA): These nonprofit agencies provide information and serve as the initial point for most fixed term RMs available in their area. Many of these agencies are also HUD-approved counseling agencies and perform the services required under the HECM demonstration program described above. The RM lenders to which they refer homeowners are sometimes too numerous to list on this summary (in AZ, CA, MA, MN, NY, NJ). These agencies are listed under the geographic area(s) they serve.

STATE SPONSORED LENDER (SSL): Montana, Connecticut and New Hampshire now offer a "split term" RM at below market interest rates to borrowers whose incomes fall under established limits. Monthly cash advances are made to borrowers for a fixed number of years; no repayment is required until the last borrower dies, sells or moves.

Prepared by: AARP/Consumer Affairs Section (Attn: Ms. Bronwyn Belling)
601 E Street, N.W.
Washington, DC 20049
(202) 434-6044 (Fax: 434-6466)
Revised December 1994

Please notify us of any corrections to this list, using the above address or telephone number.

Appendix D
Fannie Mae's Seniors' Housing Opportunities

March 1991

Fannie Mae To Test New Approaches for Financing Seniors' Housing

The graying of America has increased the demand for housing options for senior citizens—options that often must balance a desire for privacy and independence with a need to accommodate physical limitations and fixed incomes. With 40 million Americans over 60, there is an acute need for a more specialized approach to seniors' housing. Fannie Mae is asking lenders, as well as senior citizens organizations, to join us in developing and testing financing alternatives targeted to this market.

We have:

- researched the unique housing needs and preferences of senior citizens;
- evaluated the alternative housing arrangements being proposed in the marketplace;
- analyzed our mortgage eligibility and underwriting standards to highlight existing opportunities and to identify changes that would enable us to better support seniors' housing without compromising credit quality; and

- set aside $100 million to fund a demonstration project to test four promising options.

Special underwriting considerations and the demonstration project are outlined below.

Standard Underwriting Guidelines Accommodate the Older Borrower

Fannie Mae's standard underwriting guidelines take into account many factors which might demonstrate an older borrower's ability to pay. For instance, we accept several sources of personal income that are common among older borrowers. These sources of income include:

- part-time income,
- retirement income,
- social security,
- income from notes receivable and
- interest and dividends.

Fannie Mae also encourages lenders to give special consideration to regular sources of income that are nontaxable, such as disability retirement payments. The tax savings on this income may be added to the borrower's actual income for qualification purposes.

Our underwriting guidelines justify the consideration of higher debt-to-income ratios when strong offsetting factors are present. Those factors common among senior citizens are:

- a large downpayment toward the purchase of the property;
- a borrower's demonstrated ability to devote a greater portion of income to basic needs like housing expenses; or
- net worth substantial enough to evidence the borrower's ability to repay the mortgage.

Fannie Mae's Demonstration Project Will Test Other Promising Options

Fannie Mae has earmarked $100 million to fund Seniors' Housing Opportunities (SHO)—a demonstration project to test four alternative housing arrangements that have been widely discussed in the marketplace. These options, which are outlined in greater detail further on, include:

- accessory apartments,
- ECHO housing—temporary units built on a family member's property,
- homesharing and
- sale-leaseback.

Our research indicated that these housing alternatives could benefit seniors with certain needs or characteristics. We also found that those benefits could be enhanced with the adoption of several variances to our standard underwriting criteria. Lenders will recognize the sale-leaseback as a traditional transaction that enables older homeowners to remain in the homes they currently occupy. Other arrangements, such as ECHO housing, are relatively new. Fannie Mae will consider still different proposals by lenders or by public or private agencies involved in providing housing for seniors.

Project Criteria Are Flexible

We believe strongly that flexibility is critical if we are to have a lasting impact in the field of seniors' housing. Rather than defining specific requirements, we are advising lenders, as well as the public and private agencies involved in providing seniors' housing, of the types of variances that we will consider. We encourage lenders to work with public and private agencies to develop approaches like those described in this bulletin.

Qualifying criteria for SHO vary with the nature of the financing arrangement. However, two criteria are common to all:

- at least one of the parties to the transaction must be 62 years or older; and
- all proposed uses must represent a legal use of the property.

Accessory Apartments

An accessory apartment is a second, completely private living unit installed in a home designed as a single-family residence. The apartment may be used in one of two ways. In one instance, the older homeowner may desire additional income, or the security and companionship of someone living nearby. The apartment may be occupied by a relative of the homeowner, or by an unrelated tenant who may agree to provide services in return for a rent reduction. Or, an owner may install an apartment for use by one or more older relatives. An accessory apartment can be a solution for seniors who may need occasional help or who need to know that such help is nearby, but who do not wish to sacrifice independence and privacy or to impose upon that of their children.

We will consider the purchase of mortgages secured by single-family properties containing accessory apartments that meet the following criteria:

- The mortgagor—either the senior or a relative—must occupy the property as his or her principal residence.
- Fixed-rate purchase money mortgages may have loan-to-value (LTVs) ratios up to 95 percent, instead of our normal 90 percent limitation for two-family properties. Adjustable-rate mortgages (ARMs) may have LTVs up to 90 percent.
- Refinance mortgages with LTVs up to 90 percent are eligible if the loan proceeds are being used to construct the accessory apartment. Normally, the maximum LTV for refinance mortgages is 90 percent for "no cash-out" transactions and 75 percent for "cash-out" transactions.
- Maximum financing may not be offered in areas where property values are declining.
- Any mortgage amount in excess of 75 percent LTV must be covered by mortgage insurance.
- Net incremental rental income received for the accessory apartment may be included in the borrower's qualifying income. This differs from our standard underwriting guidelines, which do not permit rent from boarders to be counted as income when the mortgagor occupies a property as a principal residence.

ECHO Housing

An ECHO (Elderly Cottage Housing Opportunity) dwelling is a separate, self-contained, temporary unit built on the lot of an existing home as a residence for a relative. Like an accessory apartment, this arrangement permits family members to maintain close contact with older relatives without infringing on each other's privacy.

We will consider purchasing mortgages secured by properties with two structures—the primary single-family home and the ECHO unit—that meet the following criteria:

- Both the ECHO unit and the permanent structure must be occupied as principal residences. At least one occupant of the ECHO unit must have a family relationship with the owner of the primary residence.
- "Cash-out" refinance mortgages secured by the primary residence may have LTVs as high as 90 percent if the loan proceeds will be used to finance the construction and/or installation of an ECHO unit. Normally, the maximum LTV for "cash-out" refinances is 75 percent. We will require that the mortgage amount in excess of 75 percent LTV be covered by mortgage insurance. The LTV should be based on an appraisal of the primary residence only. The value of the ECHO unit may not be considered.
- Net incremental rental income received for the ECHO unit may be included in the borrower's qualifying income. This differs from our standard underwriting guidelines, which do not permit rent from boarders to be counted as income when the mortgagor occupies a property as a principal residence.

Homesharing

"Homesharing" is a term applied to a number of affordable housing options. Common arrangements include:

- Older homeowners sharing their homes with unrelated persons of any age. In exchange, the boarder might pay rent for room, and possibly board, and/or provide services such as housekeeping.
- Senior citizens occupying a home owned by a third party.
- Unrelated persons purchasing a home together.

Although Fannie Mae will consider any other proposal involving homesharing, we generally expect a private or public agency with experience in homesharing or homematching to participate in the program.

To make financing for homesharing alternatives more readily available, we will consider purchasing mortgages that meet the following criteria:

- Eligible mortgagors include public or nonprofit agencies experienced in seniors' services or housing. Normally, we require that mortgagors be individuals. The mortgage must represent a valid, fully enforceable lien on the security property. This is of particular concern when the mortgagor is a public agency. We will accept, on a limited basis, partnerships or corporations with demonstrated experience in the area of seniors' housing. We also will waive our limitation on the number of mortgages outstanding to one borrower.
- One- to four-family properties that will be rented to two or more older tenants are eligible.
- Mortgages secured by investment properties in a homesharing arrangement may have LTVs up to 90 percent if the mortgagor is a public or nonprofit agency, partnership or corporation. Normally, investor financing is limited to 70 percent. We will require that the mortgage amount in excess of 75 percent LTV be covered by mortgage insurance (not all mortgage insurance companies provide this coverage).
- Net incremental rental income from a boarder may be included in qualifying income when a senior homeowner is purchasing or refinancing a single-family home. Normally rent from boarders may not be considered when the mortgagor occupies a property as a principal residence.

Sale-Leaseback

With a sale-leaseback arrangement, an investor purchases the property of a senior homeowner and leases it back to the same person. This enables seniors to benefit from the sales proceeds of their homes without having to move.

To facilitate financing for sale-leaseback arrangements, we will consider mortgages that meet the following criteria:

- Eligible mortgagors include public or nonprofit agencies, and on a limited basis, partnerships and corporations, with demonstrated experience in the area of seniors' housing. Normally, we require that mortgagors be individuals. The mortgage must represent a valid, fully enforceable lien on the security property. This is of particular concern when the mortgagor is a public agency. We also will waive our limitation on the number of mortgages outstanding to one borrower.
- The maximum LTV is 90 percent, in contrast to the 70 percent limitation usually applied to investment properties. We will require that the mortgage amount in excess of 75 percent LTV be covered by mortgage insurance (not all mortgage insurance companies provide this coverage).
- The lease agreement must provide for occupancy by the seller/tenant for at least five years. Life-tenancy would be preferable.

Fixed- and Adjustable-Rate Mortgages Are Eligible

Eligible mortgages include 15- and 30-year fixed-rate mortgages, 6-month and 1-year cost of funds-indexed ARMs, and 1-year and 3-year Treasury-indexed ARMs. Because seniors often have limited potential for increased income, ARMs should be underwritten using the maximum interest rate that could be in effect at the end of the first year. Pricing will be the same as that for Fannie Mae's standard products.

Here's How To Participate

To participate in Fannie Mae's demonstration program, submit your proposal to the marketing staff in your lead regional office. Your proposal should include specific project descriptions and should specify any requested variances to our standard requirements. Six-month standby commitments are available through your regional negotiator. There is no fee for the standby commitment.

On a variance basis, we also will consider purchasing individual mortgages that are not a part of the Senior's Housing Opportunities described above, but offer another viable approach to seniors' housing. Call your regional office for more information.

Southeastern Regional Office
(404) 365-6129
(404) 365-6102

Midwestern Regional Office
(312) 368-6279
(312) 368-6352

Southwestern Regional Office
(214) 770-7345
(214) 770-7338

Western Regional Office
(818) 568-5140
(818) 568-5141

Northeastern Regional Office
(215) 575-1411
(215) 575-1419
(215) 575-1440

Index

A

Accessory apartments, 78, 171–72
Accountant, 57–59
  seminars and, 93
Activity bar chart (sample), 114
Adjustable-rate mortgages, 172, 175
Agency, 68–72
  buyer, 69, 70–71
  dual, 71–72
  traditional, 69–70
Agency disclosure, 5
Agent
  choosing, 102
  information (example), 105
  responsibilities, 32, 49–50
Aging, state agencies on housing and, 133–45
Agreement of sale, 46
AIDS, 66
Alabama
  Aging Commission, 133
  reverse mortgage lenders, 151

Alaska
  reverse mortgages and, 152
  state agency on housing, 133
American Housing Survey, 90–91
American Samoa, 133
Arizona
  reverse mortgage lenders, 152
  state agencies on housing and aging, 134
Arkansas
  reverse mortgage lenders, 152
  state agencies on housing and aging, 134
  state housing finance authority, 147
Asbestos, 127
Attorney, 55–57
  criteria for choosing, 57
  seminars and, 93

B

Best interests, 48, 52
Best Lawyers in America, The, 57, 61

Bureau of the Census, 90–91
Business philosophy, 98
Buyer agency, 70–71

C

Calendar of events (sample), 106
California
  reverse mortgage lenders, 152–54
  state agencies on housing and aging, 134
Census tracts, 90
Certified Life Underwriters, 59
Children, and housing laws, 66
Civil Rights Acts, 66
CLOs, 30
Closing
  costs, estimated (sample), 118
  date, 128
Colorado
  reverse mortgage lenders, 154
  state agencies on housing and aging, 134
Communication, 44
Community health check, 96
Compassion, 21–25

Computer-generated support materials, 44
Computer loan origination, 30
Condition, of property, 37–39, 72
Condominiums, and reverse mortgages, 167
Connecticut
    reverse mortgage lenders, 155
    state agencies on housing and aging, 134
    state housing finance authority, 148
Contracts, and timing, 46
Cooperatives, and reverse mortgages, 167
Cost of living, 18–19
Credibility, and compassion, 21–25
Curb appeal, 39

D

Debt, attitudes toward, 74–75
Delaware
    reverse mortgage lenders, 155
    state agencies on housing and aging, 135
Demographics, 8–9, 74, 90–91
Disclosure
    agency, 5, 68
    property, 5, 39, 72
Discrimination, 14, 66–68
Distance, of final move, 12–13
District of Columbia
    agencies on housing and aging, 135
    reverse mortgage lenders, 155
Diversity, of over-55 clients, 25
Dual agency, 71–72

E

Early retirement, 8
ECHO housing, 78, 171, 172–73
Education, of seller, 24–25

Elderly Cottage Housing Opportunity. *See* ECHO housing
Emotional attachments, 75
Empathy, 24
Environment, 17
Equity, 8
Estate planner, 59–61
    criteria for recommending, 61
    seminars and, 93
Exclusive services (sample), 107
Expected average mortgage interest rate, 85
Expertise, 25

F

Fair housing, 65–68
Family
    importance of, 13–15
    participation, in transaction, 53, 54–55
Fannie Mae's Seniors' Housing Opportunities, 78, 169–76
    accessory apartments, 171–72
    adjustable-rate mortgages, 175
    demonstration project, 170–71
    ECHO housing, 172–73
    fixed-rate mortgages, 175
    homesharing, 173–74
    new financing approaches, 169–70
    participation in, 175–76
    project criteria, 171
    sale-leaseback, 174–75
    standard underwriting guidelines, 170
Federal Housing Administration, 85. *See also* Home Equity Conversion Mortgages
FHA-Insured RM Lenders, 151, 166
Fiduciary relationship, 68–69
15-year, fixed-rate mortgage,

79–80
55 or over one-time exclusion, 58
Finance authorities, housing, 147–50
Financial profile review process, 60
Financing options, 73–80
    attitudes and attributes, 74–77
    strategies and tools, 77–78
    types of households and, 73
    younger seniors and, 79–80
Fixed-rate mortgages, 79
    Fannie Mae Seniors' Housing Opportunities and, 175
    purchase money mortgages, 172
Fixed Term RM Lender, 167
Florida
    reverse mortgage lenders, 155–56
    state agencies on housing and aging, 135
Forms, proliferation of, 24, 27
Fourteenth Amendment, 66
Freedom Home Equity Partners, 168
Fuel tanks, buried, 127
Furniture buy-outs or consignments, 62

G

Georgia
    reverse mortgage lenders, 156
    state agencies on housing and aging, 135
Glitches, 128–29
Guam, 136

H

Handbook 4235, 167
Handicapped persons, 66
Hawaii

reverse mortgage lenders, 156

state agencies on housing and aging, 136

Health and health care, 18, 58

Health check, community, 96

Health walks, 94-95

Home condition, considering, 37-39

Home equity, 8

Home Equity Conversion Mortgages, 83, 85-86, 151, 166

Home inspections, 29, 126-27

Homeownership status, older Americans, 9-11

Homeowner's homework, 119

Homeselling process, 122

Homesharing, 78, 173-74

House calls, 44

Housing, state agencies on, 133-45

Housing finance authorities, 147-50

HUD

-approved counseling agencies, 85, 167

Field Office, 167

I

Idaho

reverse mortgage lenders, 156

state agencies on housing and aging, 136

Illinois

reverse mortgage lenders, 157

state agencies on housing and aging, 136

state housing finance authority, 148

Income

Fannie Mae's Seniors' Housing Opportunities and, 170

older Americans', 8, 10

Independent Counseling Agency, 168

Indiana

reverse mortgage lenders, 157

state agencies on housing and aging, 137

Inflation, 58

Initial contacts, 34

Inspections, 29, 126-27

Iowa

reverse mortgage lenders, 157

state agencies on housing and aging, 137

K

Kansas

reverse mortgage lenders, 157

state agencies on housing and aging, 137

Kennedy, Danielle, 48

Kentucky, 78

reverse mortgage lenders, 158

state agencies on housing and aging, 137

state housing finance authority, 149

L

Lead paint, 127

Legal counsel, 55-57

Lender Approval and Recertification Division, HUD, 167

Life expectancies, 58

Lifestyle changes, 62

Lifestyle tour, 95-96

Line of credit option, 84, 85

Listing

considerations, 33-41

materials, 99, 119-30

paperwork, 40-41

Living costs, 18-19

Living wills, 57

Louisiana

reverse mortgage lenders, 198

M

Maine

reverse mortgage lenders, 158

state agencies on housing and aging, 138

Malls

health walks in, 94-95

prospecting in, 91

Market, over-55

identifying, 89-91

importance of, 7-19

profitability of, 1-5

prospecting, 91-96

Marketing plan (sample), 121

Market introduction, for client (sample), 101

Market time/pricing relationship, 113

Martindale Hubbell Legal Reference, 57, 61

Maryland

reverse mortgage lenders, 158

state agencies on housing and aging, 138

state housing finance authority, 149

Massachusetts

reverse mortgage lenders, 158

state agencies on housing and aging, 138

Medical benefits, 58

Michigan

reverse mortgage lenders, 159

state agencies on housing and aging, 138

Minnesota

reverse mortgage lenders, 159

state agencies on housing and aging, 139

Mississippi
    reverse mortgage lenders, 159
    state agencies on housing and aging, 139
Missouri
    reverse mortgage lenders, 159
    state agencies on housing and aging, 139
Mobile homes, and reverse mortgages, 167
Montana
    reverse mortgage lenders, 160
    state agencies on housing and aging, 139
Mortgage debt, attitudes toward, 74-75
Mortgage
    preparation, 30
    process, 31
Moving coordinator, 52, 62-63
    criteria for choosing, 63
Moving list, 130-31
Multiple unit dwellings, 167

N

Nebraska
    reverse mortgage lenders, 160
    state agencies on housing and aging, 139
Negotiating, 47-49
Nevada
    reverse mortgage lenders, 160
    state agencies on housing and aging, 140
New Hampshire
    reverse mortgage lenders, 160
    state agencies on housing and aging, 140

New Jersey
    reverse mortgage lenders, 160-61
    state agencies on housing and aging, 140
New Mexico
    reverse mortgage lenders, 161
    state agencies on housing and aging, 140
New York
    reverse mortgage lenders, 161
    state agencies on housing and aging, 141
1990 Census of Population, 90
North Carolina
    reverse mortgage lenders, 161-62
    state agencies on housing and aging, 141
North Dakota
    reverse mortgage lenders, 162
    state agencies on housing and aging, 141

O

Offer
    negotiating and, 48-49
    preparing seller for, 45-46
Ohio
    reverse mortgage lenders, 162
    state agencies on housing and aging, 141
Oklahoma
    reverse mortgage lenders, 162
    state agencies on housing and aging, 141
Oregon
    reverse mortgage lenders, 162-63
    state agencies on housing and aging, 142

    state housing finance authority, 150

P

Packers, 62
Paperwork, 27-31, 40-41
Patience, 23
Peaceful environment, 17
Pennsylvania
    reverse mortgage lenders, 163
    state agencies on housing and aging, 142
Planning, for future housing needs, 15-17
Population distribution, by age, 9
Preparedness, for move, 15, 16-17
Pricing, 35-36, 46
    comparative market analysis, 116
    importance of, 108
    introduction, for client (sample), 100
    presentation (example), 99, 111-18
    price/market time relationship, 113
    prospective buyers and, relationship between, 117
    relationship to showings, offer and sale, 110
    showing activity/pricing relationship, 114
Principal limit factor, 85
Printed communications, 36, 44
Property condition, 37-39, 72
Property disclosure, 5, 72
Property tax increases, 18
Prospecting, 91-96
    community health checks, 96
    health walks, 94-95
    lifestyle tours, 95-96
    seminars, 91-94

Puerto Rico
   reverse mortgage lenders, 163
Purchase money mortgage, 58, 82

R

Radon inspection, 29, 126–27
Realtor, choosing, 102
Reference list, sample, 103
Refinance mortgages, accessory apartments and, 172
Relationship,
   establishing, 34–39
   first visit, 35
   home condition, considering, 37–39
   initial contact, 34
   second visit, 35–37
Renovations, 38
Retirement planning, 58
Reverse annuity mortgage, 58, 73, 76, 80, 81–84. *See also* Home Equity Conversion Mortgages
   characteristics of most likely users, 83
   risks, 83, 84, 87
   tenure, term and line of credit options, 84
Reverse mortgage, 58. *See also* Reverse annuity mortgage
   lenders list (by state), 151–66
   program and service summaries, 166–67
Rhode Island
   reverse mortgage lender, 163
   state agencies on housing and aging, 142
   state housing finance authority, 150
Room planning service, 62–63

S

Sale-leaseback, 78, 174–75
Sales contract, 46
Self-insured reverse mortgage lenders, 167
Seller preparation
   for offer, 45–46
   support materials, 44
   what to expect, 43–45
Seller's checklist, 130
Seminars, 91–94
   fees, 93–94
   guest speakers, 93
   process of, 94
Senior clients
   "conventional wisdom" and, 2–4, 7
   reality of market, 9–19
Senior Olympics, 95
Seniors' Housing Opportunities. *See* Fannie Mae's Seniors' Housing Opportunities
Septic tank inspection, 127
Shopping malls
   health walks in, 94
   prospecting in, 91
Showing property, 41
   record log (sample), 120
Solitary living, 17
South Carolina
   reverse mortgage lenders, 163–64
   state agencies on housing and aging, 142
South Dakota, state agencies on housing and aging, 142
Special services provided (sample), 98
State agencies on housing and aging, 133–45. *See also under* individual states
State housing finance authorities, 147–50
State Sponsored Lender, 168
Status report, 45

Stereotypes, 2–4, 7
Support materials, 44, 97–131
   listing materials, 99, 119–31
   prelisting packet, 98, 100–110
   pricing presentation, 99, 111–18
   purpose of, 97–98

T

Tax considerations, 18–19, 58–59
Team approach, 38, 46, 51–64
   accountant, 57–59
   attorney, 55–57
   estate planner, 59–61
   family member, 54–55
   management, 64
   moving coordinator, 62–63
Telephone company, seller notification of, 130
Tennessee
   reverse mortgage lenders, 164
   state agencies on housing and aging, 143
Tenure option, 84
Termite inspection, 127
Term option, 84, 85
Testimonials (example), 104
Texas
   reverse mortgages and, 164
   state agencies on housing and aging, 143
Thirty-day homeselling process, 122
Traditional agency, 69–70
Transamerica HomeFirst, 168
Treasury bill rate, and mortgages, 79
Trust, 22
203(b)(2) limit, 167

U

Utah
    reverse mortgage lenders,
        164
    state agencies on housing
        and aging, 143
Utilities
    cost increases in, 18
    seller notification of, 130

V

Value, determining, 109
Variable-rate mortgage, 79
Vermont
    reverse mortgage lenders,
        164
    state agencies on housing
        and aging, 143

Virginia
    reverse mortgage lenders,
        165
    state agencies on housing
        and aging, 144
Virgin Islands, housing agency
    for, 144

W

Washington
    reverse mortgage lenders,
        165
    state agencies on housing
        and aging, 144
Well water, 127
West, Buddy, 92

West Virginia
    reverse mortgages and, 166
    state agencies on housing
        and aging, 144
Widowed seniors, 76
Wills, 57, 60
Wisconsin
    reverse mortgage lenders,
        166
    state agencies on housing
        and aging, 145
Wyoming
    reverse mortgage lenders,
        166
    state agency on housing,
        145